PRACTICAL BUSINESS NEGOTIATION

Practical Business Negotiation introduces university students to business negotiation as practiced in the globalized business world. There are no other textbooks that take on this topic in depth with non-native English speakers in mind. Current textbooks about negotiation tend to be dense, academic and less than practical in content. Many are demotivating to students who are not easily able to consume a few hundred pages of academic writing.

This textbook takes a step-by-step approach, providing bite-sized presentations of negotiation concepts with practical exercises that include linguistic as well as negotiation content. Explanations are reinforced with practical questions and problem solving and recent examples drawn from a business world that includes much more than North America and Europe.

William W. Baber is an Associate Professor at the Graduate School of Management, Kyoto University, Japan, where he teaches business negotiation, cross cultural management and communication. He was a marketing strategist and business attraction specialist for the Maryland State Department of Business and Economic Development, Baltimore, Maryland, USA from 1998–2005. He has worked frequently with business decision-makers from Europe, Asia and around the USA, and has accumulated rich experience in practical business negotiation.

Chavi C-Y Fletcher-Chen is a Professor at IÉSEG School of Management, Université Catholique de Lille, France, teaching practical negotiation skills, interpersonal communication applied to negotiation and e-negotiation. She has published case studies in the area of negotiation. Coming from an international business background, she has extensive experience in international marketing and conflict management through working for years in international patent, trademark and commercial law firms in the Far East. In addition, she has experience in training commercial managers in cross-cultural communication. She specializes in information communication technologies (ICTs), and has consulted for global companies.

PRACTICAL BUSINESS NEGOTIATION

William W. Baber and Chavi C-Y Fletcher-Chen

Routledge
Taylor & Francis Group

LONDON AND NEW YORK

First published 2015
by Routledge
2 Park Square, Milton Park, Abingdon, Oxon OX14 4RN

and by Routledge
711 Third Avenue, New York, NY 10017

Routledge is an imprint of the Taylor & Francis Group, an informa business

© 2015 William W. Baber and Chavi C-Y Fletcher-Chen

The right of William W. Baber and Chavi C-Y Fletcher-Chen to be identified as authors of this work has been asserted by them in accordance with the Copyright, Designs and Patent Act 1988.

British Library Cataloguing-in-Publication Data
A catalogue record for this book is available from the British Library

Library of Congress Cataloging-in-Publication Data
Baber, William W.
    Practical business negotiation / William W. Baber and Chavi C-Y Fletcher-Chen. — 1 Edition.
        pages cm
    1. Negotiation in business.   I. Fletcher-Chen, Chavi C.Y.   II. Title.
    HD58.6.B33 2015
    658.4'052—dc23
    2014044696

ISBN: 978-1-138-78147-4 (hbk)
ISBN: 978-1-138-78148-1 (pbk)
ISBN: 978-1-315-71407-3 (ebk)

Typeset in Bembo
by Apex CoVantage, LLC

Printed and bound in Great Britain by
CPI Group (UK) Ltd, Croydon, CR0 4YY

CONTENTS

FIGURES

TABLES

CASES

ACKNOWLEDGMENTS

It is important to point out that this textbook owes a debt to a variety of people who have guided the authors and contributed directly or indirectly to its development.

Those people include Chavi C-Y Fletcher-Chen, the resourceful co-author of this textbook, Peter Kesting and Remi Smolinski, both of Aarhus University, who encouraged my interest in negotiation, and Helen Lam of Athabasca University.

Additionally I want to acknowledge the many students from whom I have learned over the years. In particular I would like to thank Sean Penn for the use of the emotional client case, D. Zhang for his insistent and persistent question-asking, L. Ipsen and S. Sepstrup for allowing me to quote select data from their thesis, R. Lavoie for her Why-Why graphic, and of course numerous MBA students in Kyoto and elsewhere.

Lastly I acknowledge the patience and support of my wife and children through this project!

William W. Baber III

First of all I would like to thank William W. Baber for giving me the opportunity to collaborate with him on this textbook. Appreciation to IÉSEG School of Management for their resources and finally my husband for his understanding and encouragement.

Chavi C-Y Fletcher-Chen

INTRODUCTION

The purpose of this textbook is to put the practical knowledge and tools necessary to negotiate well in business in the hands of students.

The textbook seeks to answer practical questions like:

- What is the overall process of negotiation?
- How do you start?
- What is the sequence?
- What should you expect?
- What phrases communicate the right intention?
- How do you finish it up?
- How do you learn more about it?

The textbook uses plain English, not difficult academic English. The textbook uses many diagrams to help visually explain the processes. Technical words (jargon) are explained so that you can use them properly to communicate your plans and ideas to your team, your superiors and companies you do business with.

The processes and ideas discussed in this textbook are based on the standard practices of "Western business" institutions – practices we must understand in order to function successfully in international business. The learning points in this book will be useful in most kinds of business interactions. However, local business practices and customs must be respected and understood in order to achieve local and regional success.

This textbook will teach you basic ideas about business negotiation through reading, discussing and doing. Each section of this textbook contains one or two key points about planning, structuring, verbalizing or understanding negotiation. Using the case studies included, you will learn and practice phrases and jargon commonly used in negotiation. Additionally, you will learn the importance of understanding the other side as well as how to understand the other side.

Fundamentally, this textbook teaches that negotiation is an opportunity to create value and business opportunities. Negotiation should not be a fight to take value from another party. Negotiation should be a constructive conversation in which all parties take home at least as much value as they need. Some of that value may be distributed in a zero-sum way, but additional value should be created to replace value conceded to other parties.

By the end of this text you should be able to:

- identify and use key negotiating strategies;
- identify monetary and non-monetary interests of all parties;
- use various methods to prepare properly, including understanding your counterparts and organizing before negotiating;
- use questions to understand the goals of counterparts;
- provide and receive helpful information;
- identify and improve a BATNA;
- identify and avoid poor tactics and negotiating practices;
- engage in a mutually successful negotiation in which all parties are satisfied, and you have not unnecessarily given away value.

What kind of negotiation

The negotiation we will discuss and study in this textbook is business negotiation. There are other areas of negotiation, for example political negotiation, which we will not directly discuss. Business negotiation is largely a transparent experience with both sides openly seeking money, business opportunities and other forms of value. Political negotiation, on the other hand, is much less open and often threatened by the actions of individuals and groups who do not seek common benefit.

Process

As a practical textbook, you will learn useful "how to" processes. Here we need to be a little cautious. Cognitive psychology shows that processes are useful for simple tasks, but not for complex activities. For example, you can easily learn to turn a car left or right, to start and to stop, but these do not add up to the complicated activity of driving a car; however, after you learn turning, starting, and stopping, you are able gain the experience necessary to drive safely.

In the same way, business negotiation is a complicated procedure that cannot be put into a cookbook recipe of easy steps. You need to know why and how the process works in order to become an expert. The processes included in this textbook are therefore useful as small steps and general overall guidelines. They are not strict recipe cooking steps. Your first driving lessons are probably on a safe course or parking lot, not a fast highway. Similarly, this textbook contains exercises, examples and simulations so that you can learn by doing, even if you are not at risk of losing money or business.

Contents

Most of this text discusses approaches to resolving problems and difficulties in negotiations, or "solving problems jointly," as in the book *3D Negotiation* by Lax and Sebenius (2006) and other books broadly referred to as the Harvard Method. Part of this text is devoted to useful words, phrases, and practices that will help students become comfortable with the process of negotiating. Practical steps for problem solving, researching and designing agreements are included. A portion of this text is reserved for tactics, mainly regarding avoiding and handling aggressive tactics.

1
WHAT DO YOU WANT TO GET FROM NEGOTIATIONS?

Distributive and integrative

"What are you trying to get?" This is a key overall question to answer before beginning the planning and talking.

Your answer is likely to be "as much as possible" or "best result for all" or a combination of these two.

The following two concepts are fundamental to understanding negotiation and how negotiators think.

Distributive perspective. Negotiators try to dominate the other party because they believe they are in direct conflict with the other party over limited resources. Negotiators fight hard for their positions (specific prices or amounts) because their loss is the other side's gain. The negotiators believe there will be a clear winner and loser, but not multiple winners.

Adapted from Metcalf and Bird, 2004

Integrative perspective. Negotiators . . . believe that all parties can win through mutually beneficial solutions. Consequently, integrative negotiators take a problem-solving approach where the focus is on exchanging information in order to identify the underlying issues and interests of both sides and to generate outcomes that benefit both parties.

Negotiators reach agreement by employing creative problem-solving approaches to develop solutions that expand the size of benefits available to everyone.

Adapted from Metcalf and Bird, 2004

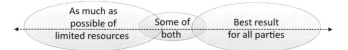

FIGURE 1.1 What are you trying to get?

Distributive thinking is useful when you must get a certain amount of limited resources for your side. In most real world business situations, however, this kind of thinking will block you from creating and sharing maximum mutual value.

Integrative thinking is useful in complex situations where you need to connect many issues and when you want to maximize the opportunities for value.

Q1: Which of these negotiations are probably distributive?
    a.   The rental price of an apartment
    b.   Deciding how Yumi, Ken and Jun will share the last piece of cake
    c.   Starting a new training camp for a winning major league baseball team in a rural area
    d.   A football star's salary with their team

Q2: Ichiro is a Japanese baseball star. He is so famous everyone recognizes him just by his first name! His main advertising contract is with Kirin beer, one of the three large beer makers in Japan. Write one short sentence about how Ichiro's agent and negotiator will probably interact with the Kirin beer company.

    _____

    _____

Q3: Which of these negotiations are probably "integrative"?
    a)   Buying a car
    b)   Arranging a meal for your hiking club (40 people)
    c)   Buying a prepared lunch
    d)   Developing the annual financial budget of a city with two million inhabitants

Q4: Write an example of a typically distributive negotiation:_____
Q5: Write an example of a typically integrative negotiation:_____
Q6: Your company is buying a division of Osaka based Kansai Kogyou (KK). The agreement is complicated, but entirely based on money. Is it distributive or integrative? _____

> Once there were two little boys and one old broken bicycle. Each one wanted the bicycle; they could not agree to share it. Eventually they started talking, and they learned that one wanted the old tires to make a catapult and the other wanted the body to make pipes. Integration of their needs and interests made it possible to distribute everything successfully.

FIGURE 1.2 Try to get more

Another basic way to think about negotiation is **Creating** and **Claiming Value**. When you claim value, you are aiming for the left side of Figure 1.1 as a distributive negotiator. When you create value, you are aiming for the right side of Figure 1.1, and beyond. Creating value is certainly integrative – you must bring many issues together, even issues not planned for negotiation, to create new value.

Example of creating new value

A manufacturer and a distributor were negotiating a typical limited distribution agreement. After some discussions, they agreed to have the distributor make a small change to the products sold in one region. Therefore, the manufacturer sold more products and the distributor gained value-added work. Both sides created new value together beyond their plans for "typical distribution."

It is a good habit to think about opportunities for creating new value from the start of a negotiation, even during the early planning phases. Movius and Susskind (2009, pp. 180–181) include a checklist for new value creation, covering topics such as looking for variation in how the parties value the same issue, the joint use of resources, differences in risk tolerance and additional issues to add to the core transaction.

Following the ideas of Movius and Susskind, negotiators should look for opportunities to create new value in the gaps where the parties cannot easily match their abilities, viewpoints, values or resources. For example, a party that sees no value in retail sales may be happy to let another party with distribution skills handle some retail work.

Along the way, parties should look for new value opportunities where skills, interests, viewpoints and abilities overlap. For example, if both parties are good at an activity, they could bring their teams together to share best practices and gain efficiency. Figure 1.3 illustrates gaps and overlaps.

Figure 1.4 provides additional practical ideas about where to search for new value opportunities in typical contracts and agreements.

Section summary

Most negotiations include sharing finite limited resources (distributive) that are connected with more complex, tangible or intangible issues (integrative).

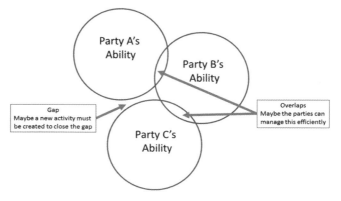

FIGURE 1.3 Creating new value: gaps and overlaps

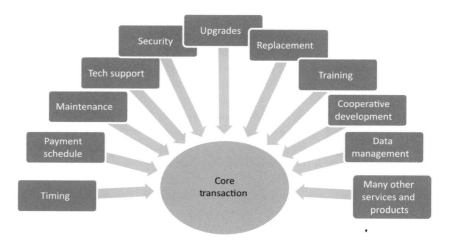

FIGURE 1.4 Where to find new value opportunities

Choosing the strategy

Five broad negotiation strategies – accommodate, collaborate, compromise, avoid and compete – are described by Lewicki, Hiam and Olander (1996) in Figure 1.5:

Negotiators use Figure 1.5 to decide which approach is best. The figure only deals with two dimensions, importance of substantive outcome (tangible and intangible gains that are at the center of a negotiation) and importance of relationship. This is a useful starting point for considering the whole negotiation and each issue within the negotiation. However, in addition to relationship and substance, there are many other factors that may have an impact on choosing the negotiation strategy.

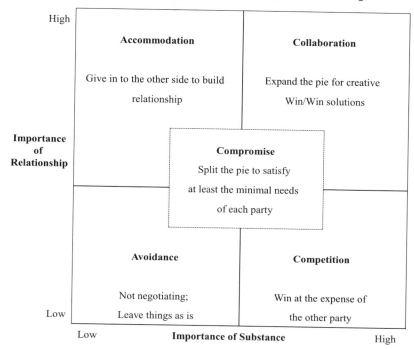

FIGURE 1.5 Choosing a negotiation strategy

Source: Lewicki, Hiam and Olander (1996)

The list of factors in Table 1.1 is adapted from Lewicki et al. (1996) as well as Ware (1980). These should be taken into consideration when choosing strategies. They include psychological, social, technical and contextual factors. These additional factors are flexible and changeable, so reassessing these factors as the negotiation develops will help you adjust strategies to match the situation.

It is helpful to select a few of the previously mentioned factors to guide your choice of strategy. Since the previously mentioned factors are relative and not absolute, we can assess them as roughly high, low or medium. Plotting the selected factors on a scale from 0–5 allows a visual determination of the most suitable strategy. For this purpose time, resources, relationship, power, trust, skills and complexity can provide an overview of the negotiation. These factors are plotted for two different negotiations in Figure 1.6.

A negotiation with high scores for many of the factors, such as the one mapped by the solid line in Figure 1.6, matches well with a competitive strategy. A negotiation with mostly low scores, such as mapped by the dotted line, is best handled with a collaborative strategy.

TABLE 1.1 Changeable factors surrounding a negotiation

Resources	Among the negotiating parties	Environment around the negotiating parties
• Scarcity of time, money, manpower, skills and other resources needed for execution of an agreement;	• Mutual respect among the negotiators;	• Complexity of issues;
• need to allocate resources precisely.	• personality of the negotiators;	• political and regulatory environment;
	• empathy among the negotiators;	• importance of maintaining a good relationship;
	• team internal relationships;	• relative power of the parties;
	• trust among the negotiators;	• uncertainty surrounding issues;
	• physical environment;	• pressure from stakeholders;
	• procedural matters;	• limited time for negotiating;
	• negotiator skill level.	• importance of outcomes.

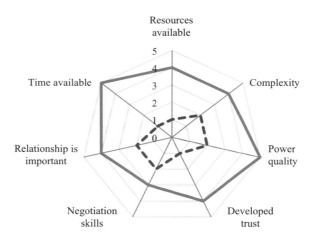

FIGURE 1.6 Compete or collaborate

Urgency, stakes and relationship

Another way to choose a strategy is to consider urgency, stakes and relationship. Urgency refers to the speed with which the organization hopes to complete the negotiation. Stakes refer to the importance of the outcome; for example, high stakes might mean survival or failure of the organization. Low stakes, however, means

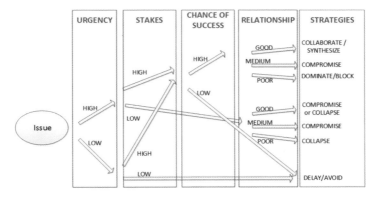

Urgency, Stakes, Chance of Success,
and Relationship as factors in choice
of negotiation strategy

FIGURE 1.7 Choosing negotiation strategies

little impact on the organization. Relationship refers to the quality of the existing relationship.

To use Figure 1.7, consider the three categories in order from left to right for each issue or for the overall negotiation. Follow the arrows based on your evaluation of the urgency, stakes and relationship. For example, if the urgency is low and stakes are low, there is no reason to immediately deal with the issue. If there is enough time (low urgency), the issue is important (high stakes) and the quality of the relationship is medium, look for compromises.

Case: Choosing the strategy

SamYeong, Co. and HoPha, Inc. are preparing a joint proposal for a construction project. SamYeong is an engineering services company with high skills in steel suspension design. HoPha specializes in installation of complex support systems. Both firms are able to organize the general construction work. There is a large amount of money and potential profit in the general construction work. These profits will improve the projected profits of the companies from merely acceptable to a much higher level. The companies do not have a history of cooperation, however they need to work together in order to win the contract for this project – there are no alternative partners. Somehow they will have to manage an agreement regarding the general construction work. Fortunately the two companies have a lot of time, as the bid will be submitted in 12 months.

Please evaluate the following:

Urgency: _____
Stakes: _____
Success chance: _____
Relationship: _____
Strategy: _____

Changing your strategy appropriately – staying flexible

A negotiation might move from competitive to collaborative as the parties interact more. For example, trust might increase, more time might become available, the importance of the relationship might change and so on. Because integrative,

TABLE 1.2 How negotiation factors change

Factors	Possible sources of change
Resources • Time, money, manpower, skills and other resources needed for execution of an agreement; • need to allocate resources with precision.	• Deadlines may become more flexible; • labor costs decrease/increase; • highly skilled staff is recruited or lost; • scope and funding change.
Among the negotiating parties • Mutual respect among the negotiators; • personality of the negotiators; • empathy among the negotiators; • team internal relationships; • trust among the negotiators; • physical environment; • procedural matters; • negotiator skill level.	• New staff; • team dynamic improves or breaks down; • counterparties know each other better; • skills improve; • new location/venue is agreed; • procedures become more comfortable/difficult; • negotiators link or delink issues in the negotiation to make them more or less flexible.
Environment around the negotiating parties • Complexity of issues; • political and regulatory environment; • importance of maintaining a good relationship; • relative power of the parties; • uncertainty surrounding issues; • Pressure from stakeholders; • limited time for negotiating; • importance of outcomes.	• Regulations become more friendly or more difficult; • political support or pressure from the back table increases/decreases; • new technology simplifies or complicates matters; • power changes; • knowledge and understanding increase/decrease; • time constraints expand or contract; • stakes increase or decrease.

collaborative negotiations tend to create more value for all parties, it is best to attempt to move a negotiation from competitive to collaborative. The opposite is true as well – a collaborative negotiation can break down into a competitive one as deadlines approach and parties feel the pressure of time.

Many negotiations include issues demanding collaborative/integrative approaches as well as ones that are more distributive. Therefore, it may be useful or necessary to switch strategies. Ware (1980) suggests separating the approaches in time and space with appropriate sequencing and packaging.

Handling problem solving first in the overall sequencing of a collaborative or mixed strategy negotiation is preferable, as discussed in Chapter 4. Without an idea about the possible solutions before taking on the competitive issue, the chance of confusing the negotiation partners and souring the communication increases.

Power

There are three kinds of power in a business negotiation, BATNA power, coercive power and perceived power. BATNA power is described in Chapter 3, and it consists of the ability to walk away if a deal is not attractive enough. Coercive power is rarely experienced in the business world in countries with sound legal systems. Often this kind of power comes from organizations or individuals in authority that can demand bribes or threaten serious consequences with no danger to themselves. Coercive power may also come from organizations that have a monopoly. Monopoly or near-monopoly organizations have the unbeatable BATNA that counterparties cannot choose to walk away. An example would be a government monopoly on a natural resource such as Precious Minerals Marketing Corporation in Ghana, which has authority as the sole legal purchaser of the output of small gold mines. There is no legal alternative to compliance with their demands.

The last kind of power, perceived power, comes from the perception that one side has a dominant position. One party may promote the idea that they are powerful, but the "power" can only have impact if the other party believes it and reacts to it. In other words, this kind of power is only real if others believe it. Parties with this kind of power might include a company that is dominant in its industry and so well respected that suppliers and partners do not want to challenge it. An example can be found in the 2014 dispute between Amazon and some publishers (e.g. Hachette), in which Amazon controls the retail market so well that they can make demands without reacting to counteroffers.

In some parts of the world, major firms can successfully exercise perceived power based on their size, history or position in the industry. The smaller companies that supply and serve them may make statements like: "We cannot resist the will of that company because they helped found the country" or "We must agree with that company because they were founded by the king's brother decades ago." However, it is of course possible to resist such companies.

In order to fight back against any form of power, a company must show how its product or services are necessary to the more powerful company, as well as how they are different from and better than the competition. Another way to fight back of course is to improve your BATNA so that you create alternatives and escape the power of the other party. In the end, a strong BATNA will be the most help in dealing with any kind of power brought by a counterparty.

When not to negotiate at all

Some negotiations should not happen. These include for example negotiations about issues where both sides have low interest, cost is high, and there is no expected value in the relationship (see Figure 1.5). Consider the following case.

Case: The incompetent translator

Some years ago, a new translation services company in the Washington, DC area ordered a translation from English into Czech. The translation was not long, and the cost was only about $500. The translator provided the Czech text on time by email. There was only one problem: the project manager who received the text immediately recognized that it used none of the special characters from the Czech alphabet.

The Czech language uses the Latin alphabet plus several modified characters for a total of 42 characters. For example, the language uses "c" and "č", and "a" as well as "á". These special characters have different pronunciations and carry important grammatical meaning. The project manager asked the translator to put the characters in, but he refused. "The text is understandable to a Czech," he said. "It is good enough."

This was certainly true – the text was comprehensible to a Czech. However, no Czech office manager or schoolteacher would accept any writing lacking the special characters. Text of that sort would only be usable in a very informal setting. It was not "good enough". The agreement with the translator had not specified any "normal" or "special" purpose, setting or formality.

The project manager, feeling the situation was very clear, refused to pay the translator. The translator insisted on payment and threatened action in the California court system. At the same time, he lodged a complaint with the American Association of Translators (AAT), of which he was a member. AAT promptly sent a demand to the project manager for payment, stating that they would blacklist the company from their services not only in California but nationwide. They did not respond to the project manager's irritated letter claiming that the text was unusable.

At this point the project manager faced a choice: try to negotiate, fight a court case 4,000 kilometers away or give up.

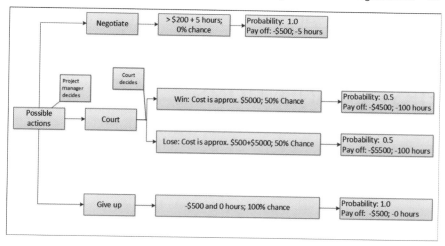

FIGURE 1.8 Decision not to negotiate

Decision time

Negotiate: The other party in the negotiation, the translator, refused to talk. The translator had successfully drawn in a powerful ally, AAT, and seemed to have their full support.

Court: Assembling the evidence against the translator would be easy. However, judges are specialists in law, not linguistics. An expert witness would cost an additional $500–$1,000. Indeed, a single plane ticket would cost at least $500. A lawyer's services would cost $2,000–$3,000. Of course the problem might not be resolved in just one visit. With experts and AAT weighing in, the court case could have gone either way – a victory or a loss.

Give up: Giving up would cost only $500 and take no time at all. There would be no concern about losing the court case and paying the costs of the other side.

The project manager's choices could be drawn as in Figure 1.8.

After considering the situation described in Figure 1.8, the project manager, with the agreement of the owner of the translation services company, gave up. The fee was paid despite the fact that the product delivered was worthless.

Do you think the project manager and owner made the right decision? Why?

_____

_____

Is this a distributive or an integrative negotiation? Please explain.

_____

_____

2
FIRST CONNECTIONS

Gaining and giving information

In the previous chapter, we encountered two basic approaches to negotiation: distributive and integrative. Distributive negotiators do not need to learn much about the other party – therefore, they typically ask only a few questions with a narrow focus and share little information about themselves. Integrative negotiators, on the other hand, ask many questions. They share much (perhaps even all) information about their positions. This section is about how queries for information may be asked and answered.

Table 2.1 provides an example: Tanba Agro is negotiating the sale and delivery of eggs to Hyogo Cake's factory.

Types of questions

Simon Hazeldine (2006), a UK business negotiator, writes that you will need to use four kinds of questions: closed, probing, open-ended and summarizing.

Closed questions

These simple questions seek specific answers to specific questions. You can ask for yes/no answers (Hazeldine, 2006, p. 63).

Probing questions

In *3D Negotiation*, Lax and Sebenius (2006) say, "If they don't like the concept, *probe*. Ask why? Why not X instead? What if Y? Then, listen actively" (p. 77).

TABLE 2.1 Constructive sharing of information

Dialog	Comment
Hyogo Cake: So basically, we need 3,000 eggs per day. Tanba Agro: OK!	"OK!" means B understands, not that B has committed to anything. Tanba Agro knows they cannot deliver the eggs all at once because of truck availability.
Tanba Agro: Your factory has an interesting process – do you use all the eggs at once?	Tanba Agro changes subject without showing the difficulty on their side by asking a general question about the factory, the process or another topic related to the cake business.
Hyogo Cake: No, we have three baking batches per day. Each time we need 1,000 eggs. Batches start at 8 AM, 11 AM and 2 PM. Tanba Agro: I see. Is it difficult to keep all those eggs until you are ready? Hyogo Cake: Yes – it takes a lot of space. Hyogo Cake: However the price is too high for us. XYZ, Corp. can deliver the eggs all at 8 AM and 3 percent cheaper. Tanba Agro: If you can take the eggs at 7:45 AM, 10:45 AM and 1:45 PM, we can decrease our offer by 2 percent.	Now Tanba Agro knows it might be possible to deliver the eggs at two or three times during the workday. Tanba Agro also now knows that Hyogo Cake might like to have the eggs arrive at three times. Tanba Agro can use this information to save money . . . or to offer Hyogo Cake a discount. Note that Tanba Agro's discount does not have to be as big as XYZ's because the delivery schedule is convenient for Hyogo Cake.

These are used to explore a point the other side has made. They allow you to drill further into what has been said so that you can understand it in more detail.

Examples include:

"What makes you say that?"

"In what way do you think . . . ?"

"How do you mean?"

"Why do you bring that up?"

A useful probing technique is to use "echo questions". An echo question is where you use the last word or few words of what the other party says as a probing question.

An example:

"We need a significant investment."

"Significant investment?"

In this example, you are probing further to discover how the other party defines "significant investment."

Source: Hazeldine, 2006, p. 64.

Why do you think that "echo questions" are effective?

_____

What do both sides learn from an echo question?

_____

In the following text, Hazeldine suggests also using broader questions that invite general exchanges of information.

Open questions

These are broad, diagositc questions that encourage the other paerty to talk about their situation. Open questions usually start with words such as what, when, why how, where, who and which, and usually result in a multi-word or sentence answer.

Examples would include:

"What do you want to change about your current situation?"
"You have mentioned you have some concerns. What are they?"

Open questions are used to gather information and closed questions are used to clarify what you discover and to get specific answers and commitments.

Hazeldine, 2006, p. 64

What is the benefit of asking open questions?

_____

In which situation during a negotiation would you ask an open question?
   a. At the beginning of negotiations
   b. When you want specific facts
   c. When you are unclear about a general idea
   d. When you are just finishing up negotiations

What kind of question would you ask after hearing, "Our company can deliver 2,000 units"?
   a. Closed
   b. Open
   c. Probing
   Write the question you might ask:
   _____?

Return to the negotiation between the egg supplier and the cake maker at the beginning of this section. What additional questions should you ask? Develop two questions Tanba Agro could ask Hyogo Cake.

a. _____

b. _____

When asking questions to identify problem points, use the inconsistency trap to learn about the other side and their understanding of the issues. To use the inconsistency trap, first ask, then listen, and then rephrase the question and ask again. Compare the answers to each other and to your sources of information to look for points that you do not understand. These points may be difficult to understand because information is poorly explained, the counterparties have hidden the information or because they have not noticed the need for the missing information.

Summarizing

See the Verbal signals section of Chapter 6 for more on this.

Section terminology

Probe: to explore and push for deeper, specific information

Commit: agree to expend money, time and other resources with full intent to complete

Diagnostic question: a question for learning general information

Inconsistency: information that is not the same as it was when first presented

Section summary

> Ask questions to gain information and build your understanding.

Relationships

In the previous section, we saw how a negotiator can ask questions to learn about the overall situation, the needs of the other party and to find ways to improve an offer in order to increase the likelihood of agreeing. Asking questions and answering questions can also help build a relationship. Fundamentally, negotiations should lead to a successful business transaction or avoidance of a bad one. But just completing one transaction is not the greatest success. The negotiation partners could benefit from building a relationship of confidence and mutual accessibility that leads to more transactions in more areas of business – that is real success. We can arrive at real success through relationships built on reciprocity, empathy and perspective taking.

Reciprocity through getting and giving

When someone tells you something, shares information with you or gives you something, you should give something in return. This is called reciprocity. Returning information or some helpful action will build and improve the relationship among the parties (Cellich and Jain, 2004). Sharing information often helps build confidence and relationships while providing the information necessary to create a good result.

Sharing information is the most common way of building relationships through reciprocity when working with companies culturally rooted in the Western world. Other parts of the world find reciprocity and build relationships through giving gifts. The gift may be an item such as expensive wine or a local specialty, or it may take the form of a favor for the other parties. In business negotiations, it may be a concession given early in the talks. Giving the gift or concession or doing the favor places a burden on the other parties to respond similarly. Just as with shared information, the pressure to respond appropriately is strong, and failing to respond appropriately may damage the relationship. This kind of interaction based on gifts and favors is part of the concept of *guanxi* in China, *ongi* and *kankei* in Japan, and may be familiar to many cultures of East and Southeast Asia in particular.

When dealing with a culture you are unfamiliar with, use very knowledgeable local people to help you prepare for the kind of reciprocity in that region. The following quote from Thams, Liu and von Glinow (2013, p. 466) is on target: ". . . although there might be some universal principles governing reciprocity, people in different cultures embrace reciprocity differently".

Reciprocity decreases tension

An air of tension can also be created by unknown factors. For example, you may never have met the people you will be negotiating with before, and this can lead to feelings of uncertainty. You can reduce the tension by remembering that your key focus . . . is to find out what the other party wants, and to communicate what you want.

Hazeldine, 2006, p. 60

However, if one party gives a small concession and expects a much better concession in return, the relationship and the negotiation will deteriorate (Cellich and Jain, 2004). If you have been given a small concession and feel pressure to give a larger concession in return, you must either get another concession or carefully consider the size and value of the concession you might give. Positive reciprocity can help the constructive exchange of information and ideas. Negative reciprocity

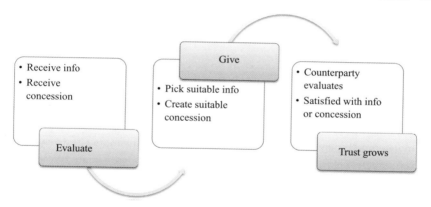

FIGURE 2.1 The cycle of sharing

(i.e. responding aggressively to aggressive actions) results in unequal sharing, damaged relationships and failed negotiations.

> How can you manage reciprocity in order to comfortably share information without losing control or not receiving reciprocal information from the other party?

Reciprocity, whether based on exchanging information or placing obligations on other parties, works because it is a widely accepted norm. Under usual conditions, most people and organizations will share information cautiously at first, and then more openly. The sharing is a process that builds trust and confidence. Be a little cautious: it is possible for a negotiation partner to abuse the reciprocity process. If the other side does not share, then you should consider a different approach or a different partner. You must be sure that the other side is sharing quality information and concessions. If you give too much too soon, you may learn too late that your negotiation partner is not working with you constructively.

Let's go beyond understanding needs to understanding interests. To do so we need empathy – the ability to recognize the feelings and thinking of others. We can use empathy to understand the reasons for the choices made by counterparties.

Section summary

Reciprocity helps build relationships and make them deeper. Relationships improve business outcomes.

Empathy

Tough or with feeling?

> Many people feel that they must choose between being assertive and being empathic – being "hard" or being "soft." But that's a false choice. Showing empathy about your counterpart's interests, perceptions, and constraints may make him or her more open to providing you with useful information. The more empathically you understand your counterpart, the more effectively you can design value-creating deals and the better positioned you are to claim a full share of that value.
>
> *3D Negotiation*, Lax and Sebenius, p. 216

Empathy is a way to improve negotiation outcomes by:

*   understanding the negation partner's values;
*   increasing mutual gains and satisfaction;
*   avoiding ethical errors.

Understanding leads to improved results, possibly for all sides. Your values may be different from the values of the other sides in the negotiation. Using empathy, you can identify the differences and perhaps more easily create solutions that protect your values as well as theirs. If the other sides cannot protect their values, they are more likely to leave the negotiation or seek new partners for future projects.

Assertiveness is often an opposite behavior to empathy. Assertiveness means putting pressure on the other sides to accept your position. Assertiveness of this sort may damage a negotiation by limiting the opportunities for other or all sides to make gains together. On the other hand, assertiveness also means getting your ideas into the conversation. Failing to get your ideas on the table will not benefit any parties.

As empathy and understanding increases, the negotiation partners will have more opportunities to maximize mutual gains, not just their own gains. As the gains of all sides increase, satisfaction is likely to increase. Importantly, empathy can help you avoid ethical mistakes like improperly explaining risks or value related to the negotiation or inappropriately taking an asset that has particularly high value attached to it by one of the other negotiation partners.

Empathy in some cultures may include additional generally positive feelings. For example, in Japan, businesspeople are often sensitive to the feeling of *en* (縁), also called *wetto*, a notion of compatibility, likability and vague potential for good results (DeMente, 2004). This feeling can impact business decisions including negotiations, contracts and follow up. The feeling of *en* is part of Japanese empathy and therefore part of relationship building in Japan. Sensitivity to creating and building culturally specific kinds of empathy is important for intercultural negotiators.

There are many ways to build empathy, but negotiators must be careful to do so in ways that match the expectations of the other sides. In any case, a commonly used approach is to show that you share identities with the other parties. Some identities that are widely shared include being parents, sports interests, fields of study, employment history and so on.

In summary, it sounds like empathy is a great thing to develop. But it is possible for empathy to create too much sympathy? After all, you might not want to explain to your boss or your shareholders that you left resources unclaimed out of sympathy. Research has found that empathy tends to increase shared gains (Galinsky, Maddux, Gilin and White, 2008) but statistically significant gains were made by another approach: perspective taking.

Section summary

> Empathy means understanding the interests and values of the other party. It helps create positive value and improves the outcome of the negotiation. It is not appropriate, however, to become too understanding.

Perspective taking

In this approach, negotiators try to understand the goals and difficulties in a negotiation from the point of view of other sides. However, they concentrate on the desired targets and goals more than the feelings of other sides. Galinsky et al. (2008, p. 382) used the phrase, "Try to understand what they [the other side] are thinking in their situation." Perspective taking resulted in greater joint gains and individual gains.

Case: Professor's patent

> Suppose that you are trying to negotiate the use of a patented process for your startup company. You do not have much money, so you prefer to pay a royalty as sales develop in the future instead of buying the patent outright. On the other side of this negotiation is a professor who is near retirement and currently working at a university in Malaysia. What do you think might be the perspectives of that professor? Taking his perspective, write down what he might be thinking about this deal:
>
> _____
> _____
> _____
>
> Compare your ideas with another student and be prepared to discuss with the group.

Review of relationship building

Please talk to your partner(s) and try to answer these questions:

> Why should you try to build relationships? How can you build positive relationships?

> **Situation:** You are in South America working on an acquisition of intellectual property. How can you build a relationship and empathy with the other party? Please write your ideas here:

But . . .

Do not expect all negotiations to result happily in future business opportunities. Here are examples of negotiations that will probably not lead to repeat business:

1.   You buy a house you expect to live in for at least the coming 20 years.
2.   You complain about poor products that your company will not need again.
3.   You disagree about the cost with a taxi driver in a foreign city.
4.   You buy services for a one-time conference overseas that your company will organize.

In the previous situations, is it sensible to spend time and energy to build relationships? Explain your answers:

1.
2.
3.
4.

Why build relationships

> Each side of the relationship should be developing plans that incorporate the other's interests into those plans. Without doing so, a long term relationship entails the disadvantage of closing off options, without accruing the benefits of the longer term commitment.
>
> (Sheppard, 2003, p. 268)

Which sentence best summarizes the previous paragraph?

a. Long term relationships must be carefully limited to avoid troubles.
b. Help the other side make their plans successful so that you can keep useful options available in the future.
c. Be sure to think long term so you can negotiate more in the future.

Sheppard (2003) also wrote, "Without mutual development, long-term relationships have no value." Do you agree? Please explain:

_____

_____

The other party tells you . . .	You reciprocate with . . .
they have new machinery but it may not work well for the first month.	_____
they are worried about getting enough workers in time.	_____
they can speed up delivery to meet your tough schedule.	_____

Lax and Sebenius (2006, p. 216) also say, "You are empathic when you try to understand the interests and motivations of the other side. You are assertive when you make your interests and demands clearly known to the other side." Is it ever useful to be assertive? Why or why not?

_____

_____

_____

Section summary

Considering a situation from the perspective of other parties is less about emotional insight than about their material interests, goals and strategies.

Impression management

At the start of your relationship with the other parties in a negotiation, and at later times, you may want to manage or control your relationship. You can manage the impression that you make in a variety of ways. You communicate your image on three levels: to the organization (macro), to other teams (meso), and to other individuals (micro). It is of course possible to communicate a different image on each level, and to change your approach as the relationship develops. Some general approaches to impression management at the team and individual levels are discussed further.

TABLE 2.2 Impression management approaches

Approach	Advantages	Disadvantages
Tough	Other parties may decrease their expectations from the start.	Other parties may react with similar tough behavior, leading the negotiations directly into deadlock or poor outcomes. See the section "Playing the hard card first" in Chapter 7.
Nice	Interactions start with a positive tone. Positive moves tend to be rewarded with positive responses.	May lead the aggressive parties to increase their demands if they perceive your image as soft.
Technical	Shows a willingness to consider technical issues and complex solutions.	If the other parties are not strong on technology, they may become less comfortable with your side.
Trusting	Other parties may share their information more confidently. A better information flow may help you make strategies and decisions. It may also lead to better relationships.	Counterparties may attempt to take advantage of perceived naiveté.
Cautious	Other sides may be cautious about making high demands.	Other parties may not share information or may not make matching concessions if they feel you are too cautious.
Corporate	A highly professional attitude may make others feel confident in your abilities.	Some parties present themselves as anti-establishment and may feel threatened by a strongly corporate look.
Professional negotiator	If you use negotiating terminology like BATNA, reserves and so on, other trained negotiators will identify you as a trained negotiator. Shared vocabulary will make communication easier and more successful.	Untrained parties may misunderstand your terminology or feel uncomfortable. The result may be poor communication.
Flexible	Being flexible signals that you are willing to solve problems creatively.	It may also signal that you are indecisive and can be bullied.
Inflexible	No clear advantage.	Other parties may not propose creative ideas if they expect you to reject them.

Presenting yourself and your organization to other organizations, at the macro level, is generally the task of the marketing and public relations specialists in your organization. If you do not have these people on your staff, carefully coordinate your macro level image management with top managers and partners. In addition to managing the impression you make on other parties, you will need to analyze the way your negotiation partners present themselves.

Section summary

> Be aware of impressions and perceptions to manage how others feel toward you.

Satisfaction

In this section, we will be discussing satisfaction as a feeling or emotion that a negotiator has received a suitable deal, not just the minimal tangible satisfaction of their requirements. No sensible party will agree to outcomes that are poor or unsatisfying. However, intangible satisfaction can range from high to low, or even negative (dissatisfaction).

Do you think that satisfaction goes up or down in sync with tangible outcomes of the negotiation – that is, is satisfaction high if a high money goal is achieved?

What is the value of satisfaction? If we can show that a negotiator can be satisfied with a deal that has less value than a perfect deal, it means that the negotiator will trade tangible value for his or her own intangible satisfaction. Therefore, a skillful negotiator will seek to build intangible satisfaction while keeping some extra tangible value. Clearly we can only manage this in integrative negotiations, but not in purely distributive negotiations. Here is how it works:

What is the future after satisfaction comes into a deal? According to Curhan, Elfenbein and Xu, (2006), individuals who were very satisfied just after a negotiation were more likely later to intend to continue the business relationship. Objective

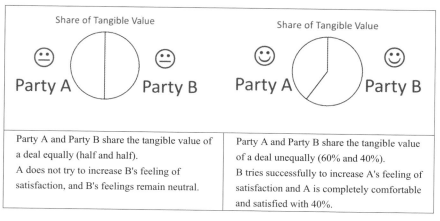

Party A and Party B share the tangible value of a deal equally (half and half). A does not try to increase B's feeling of satisfaction, and B's feelings remain neutral.	Party A and Party B share the tangible value of a deal unequally (60% and 40%). B tries successfully to increase A's feeling of satisfaction and A is completely comfortable and satisfied with 40%.

FIGURE 2.2 Impact of satisfaction on value sharing

TABLE 2.3 Creating satisfaction

Category	Write out some practical ideas for creating feelings of satisfaction in each of the four categories from Curhan et al.
How the other parties feel about themselves during the negotiation process	
How fair the negotiation process seems to the other parties	
How the other parties feel about the relationship with you and your team	
Measurable issues in the negotiation	

measures (such as tangible outcomes) had no impact on plans to continue a business relationship or not! Therefore, the benefit of making the other sides feel satisfied is not only (possibly) increased tangible gain, but also a greater chance of future deals. The value of future deals? Possibly unlimited! Curhan et al. (2006) described four ways to view the development of satisfaction in a negotiation:

- how the negotiation made us feel about ourselves;
- whether the negotiation process seemed fair;
- whether we've developed a productive working relationship with our counterparts;
- measurable gains and losses.

The first three in the previous list can only be described as feelings – these are subjective. Because they are subjective and difficult to measure, a skillful negotiator can actively influence those feelings. What can you do to develop satisfaction in the other negotiating parties?

Regarding the last item Table 2.3, measurable issues, it may be necessary to show that these have been distributed appropriately among the negotiating parties. Be prepared to demonstrate fairness. However, humans tend to attach emotional value even to things that are concretely measurable and countable, so it may be possible to influence feelings about these "facts" despite demonstrating the actual breakdown.

Section summary

> Try to build satisfaction into the negotiating process because it is more likely to lead to future business opportunities than simply exchanging concessions. Work on relationships as much or more than tangible outcomes to build satisfaction in all parties.

Relationship building at the table

At the beginning of this section, we read Lax and Sebenius' idea that empathy is almost necessary for creating new value and successful negotiation. Do you and your partners agree? Specifically what can we do at the negotiating table? Someday you may have the experience of suddenly going into a negotiation situation with counterparts you do not know. In that case, be friendly:

- smile, but show earnest intent (smiling is not appropriate in all business cultures);
- make small talk (choose appropriate topics);
- listen carefully to their small talk (show respect);
- learn about them (listen carefully, build empathy, take their perspective);
- ask them questions (listen to the answers and learn);
- share information (start the reciprocity process, communicate visually and verbally).

Swaab, Postmes, Neijens, Kiers and Dumay (2002) found in their research that using visualizations (e.g. graphics, diagrams and animations) increased satisfaction among negotiating parties; therefore, communicate using graphic images.

Active listening is the term widely used for good listening skills. Active listening requires showing that you are listening by reacting with appropriate verbal and body language signals. In some cultures, this might mean the correct use of interjections, for example ah, uh huh, mm, so and similar words when suitable. Body language response might include nodding, leaning forward, eye contact, etc. However these signals of active listening are a little different around the world. Try to use learn the correct ones for the people you are interacting with.

To summarize, negotiators need to listen and ask and listen again in order to build relationships. That process can happen away from the negotiating table and outside the office experience, before and after the actual negotiating. Never hesitate to talk to a person and listen to them. With most Europeans, North and South Americans, and people from many other cultures, you can walk directly to a person, greet them and talk. In other parts of the world where behavior is more formal, adjust your approach to the standard local behaviors.

Game theory

In the well-known prisoner's dilemma game, there are two strategies: cooperate or defect. If the game is repeated, both sides easily see the value of cooperating. Cooperation leads to greater value for all parties. The same is true in negotiation – if one side shares information and the other side shares information, both will find that sharing information is rewarding. The rewards include the creation of knowledge and trust as well as increased opportunities to create new value.

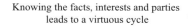

Knowing the facts, interests and parties
leads to a virtuous cycle

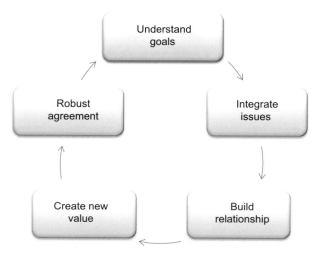

FIGURE 2.3 Virtuous cycle of knowing

Trust is the expectation that other parties will not defect. Developing trust means an evolution of events that lead to trust. That evolution can happen in the pattern illustrated in the following graphic.

Figure 2.3 has no beginning or end. It repeats with better results from greater repetitions.

Section summary

Actively build relationships because it will help the negotiation and information exchange flow smoothly.

3
CORE NEGOTIATION CONCEPTS

Anchoring effect

Lax and Sebenius explain the anchoring effect in *3D Negotiation* (2006, pp. 187–190). They found that experienced professionals receiving the same information, except for price, would suggest prices close to the first offer from the other party, even if their previous price information were very different. Therefore, Lax and Sebenius conclude that the first party to suggest a price gains an advantage. The authors also say that the price proposed must seem reasonable to the other parties because an excessive price would make the proposer seem foolish. Additionally, providing a clear compact reason for the price at the time you propose it may strengthen the anchoring effect.

A practical conclusion would be to try to be the first party to propose a price; however, the price should not be outrageous and should include some reason or explanation. Lax and Sebenius (2006, p. 187) say, " . . . make an offer *just above* the most they'd be willing to pay." Then, you can move down without losing much of the potential total value.

Example

One of the authors used to work for a business research company that specialized in Russian (then Soviet) business in 1989–1992. We had to negotiate prices for market research and information. If we were expecting a price between $5,000 and $8,000, we were shocked to hear an offer of $14,000. The offering party seemed foolish to us and we would look for another provider. In time, we learned to start the conversation with a low, but reasonable, price.

Q: What if you cannot anchor the price conversation?

A: Anchoring has its biggest effect on negotiators who are not aware of it. If you are aware of the anchor, you can re-anchor with your preferred price range. You can try to re-anchor immediately or later. You can do it bluntly or by linking issues that explain why your new anchor is sensible.

Q: What if both sides know about anchoring and try to anchor early?

A: _____

_____

Section summary

> Try to name the price first. This point is not important if the price range is limited or if price is a low priority issue.

BATNA

The abbreviation BATNA means "best alternative to negotiated agreement" and is also called a "No-Deal Option". BATNA is what you will/must do because of failing to negotiate an agreement. Before you start negotiating, it is important to know what will happen if the negotiation collapses:

Will you go bankrupt?	Will the other side go bankrupt?
Will you get fired?	Will the other party get fired?
Do you have another possible partner?	Do they have another possible partner?
Do you have time to find a new partner?	Do they have time to find a new partner?
Can either party do the work/create the product alone?	

Before the negotiation starts, prepare to understand what the negotiation choices are so you can have the best possible BATNA. A typical (good) BATNA could be having an alternative company to negotiate with.

Example: Company X makes electronic toys and wants a faster chip, but company Y only sells faster chips for an extremely high price. In this case, X must walk away. Also, Y must walk away. This is clearly a failure for both! We hope that X had already started talking with another chipmaker. We hope that Y had already started talking with another electronics maker.

Sometimes there may be more than one possible alternative to negotiating. In that case, it makes sense to consider which alternatives are better or worse. Identifying your worst alternative to negotiated agreement (WATNA) may be helpful in avoiding that result and assessing the importance of negotiating; another approach is thinking about the most likely alternative to negotiated agreement (MLATNA) (Fisher, Ury and Patton, 1991). The "most likely" result is more specific than the general notion of BATNA and can help you eliminate "best" results from your planning that might really be unlikely.

Balance

> In any negotiation, you and the other parties involved face a fundamental and ongoing choice: between staying and walking . . .
>
> This is the *deal/no-deal* balance. On one side of the balance you have the proposed deal; on the other, you have your "walk away option" . . . or BATNA.
>
> *3D Negotiation*, Lax and Sebenius, p. 27

It is extremely important to know (or estimate) the BATNA of the other negotiator(s). Is their BATNA so strong that they can walk away from the negotiating table? Is it very weak? If they have a weak BATNA, you should be able to improve your negotiating results. The following short case is about a Japanese company that was planning to buy a division (not all) of an American company.

Case: Help! We can't stop!

> During a two-year process, negotiations to buy a part of a US company stopped several times as the Japanese company rebuilt and strengthened consensus inside their company. When a European firm unexpectedly made a bid on the entire American business, the Japanese firm suddenly had to choose to complete the transaction or quit.
>
> At the last moment, [the American company started to] think again about the Japanese side's no-deal option. They quickly reviewed other options open to the Japanese firm and confirmed their undesirability. Having worked through a grueling consensus process, virtually everyone at the Japanese company . . . was deeply committed to doing this deal.
>
> Now, rather than face the extreme organizational costs of "losing," the Japanese firm agreed to pay an extraordinarily high amount for the firm.
>
> Adapted from *3D Negotiation*, Lax and Sebenius, pp. 89–90

Questions

1. In the previous section, do you think the Japanese company had a good BATNA?
2. Compare the BATNA of the US company before and after the Europeans made an offer. How did the US BATNA change?
3. How would you try to improve the BATNA of the Japanese company?
4. Write, in less than 20 words, the key error of the Japanese side.

_____

5. Should you tell your BATNA? Why or why not?

_____
_____
_____
_____
_____

Consider Figure 3.1. Did the Japanese firm in the previous case make this kind of error?

Figure 3.2 shows another way of understanding this error.

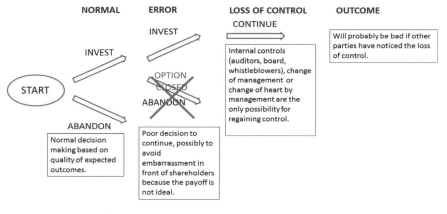

FIGURE 3.1 In too deep – decision tree

Do you agree?

Yoshiaki Fujimori, President and CEI of JS Group Corp was quoted in Bloomberg news in January 2015 on negotiating:

> Fujimori said he almost pulled out of early negotiations to buy Grohe after disagreeing on price and will always keep the option of walking away from an acquisition.

" . . . don't put yourself in a position that you must make a deal no matter what," he said.

Sato and Urabe, 2015. p. 1.

Your reaction to this statement:

_____

_____

The notion of not being able to exit a project that is developing poorly is described in the Japanese context by DeMente (2004, pp. 21–22). According to DeMente, an organization may find quitting to be too upsetting, and therefore they feel forced to commit resources even after failure has become obvious.

For more about strategic negotiation errors, see Appendix IV.

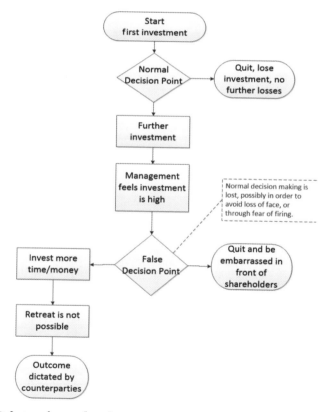

FIGURE 3.2 In too deep – flowchart

Section summary

> Develop a strong BATNA so that you can leave a negotiation that is not going well.

Understanding and misunderstanding interests

Be sure your ideas about the counterparties match the facts about their real interests. In Figure 3.3, we can see the obvious problem when ideas about the counterparty are incorrect.

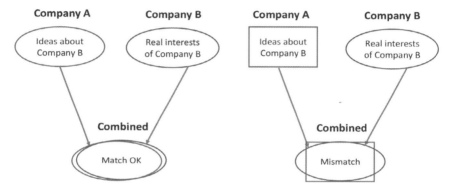

When ideas and reality about interests are correct, there will be a good match.
When interests are misunderstood, the parties will have trouble coming to agreement.

FIGURE 3.3 Interests – match v. mismatch

Source: Adapted from Raiffa, 2002.

Case: Chinalco and Rio Tinto – misunderstanding of interests

Chinalco and Rio Tinto, 2009: A Chinese/Australian business deal that could have seen the creation of a stable, diverse, multinational mining and metals company failed because the parties misunderstood some of the interests.

With strong reserves of ore in Australia and a strong market in China, the deal seemed sensible from a business viewpoint. Moreover, Rio Tinto was looking for opportunities to get cash in order to decrease its debt. Chinalco, the Chinese aluminum processor, already owned 9 percent of Rio Tinto and was willing to pay for more. Chinalco attempted to gain another 9 percent by quickly buying shares. They did this discreetly, buying on Friday in European markets. With the larger share, Chinalco would have placed two directors on Rio Tinto's board.

But the deal collapsed. In the end it was the Australian government, not Rio Tinto, regulators or shareholders, which blocked the deal for political reasons.

Beliefs about interests

TABLE 3.1 Mistaken beliefs, Chinalco and Rio Tinto case

Chinalco was incorrectly thinking that . . .	Australian Government was incorrectly thinking that . . .
• The Australian government is not important in this process; • The Australian government will not be worried about our breaking the 15 percent share limit for foreign ownership; • The Australian government will not see a threat in the presence of two directors picked by a Chinese partner; • The Australian government will not care that Chinalco is majority owned by the Chinese government; • Rio Tinto can influence the government enough to protect the deal; • If we do it quietly but inform them quickly, there will be no problem.	• Chinalco wanted to direct Rio Tinto's resources only into China; • The Chinese government made the decision to gain more shares of Rio Tinto; • The quick move to gain shares was the start of a longer campaign to gain more shares and power; • ChinaAlco's shares would make it impossible for Rio Tinto to develop as a globalized leading Australian company.

TABLE 3.2 Real interests, Chinalco and Rio Tinto case

Chinalco	Australian
• Diversification of Chinalco; • Gain experience with a respected foreign business; • Gain some control (but not dominant) over supplies from Australia. • Summary: Wanted to diversify Chinalco from aluminum.	• Strong interest in sticking to the 15% foreign ownership limit; • Strong interest in developing a powerful Australian company; • Felt it was necessary to discuss such developments in the public media (the political leaders were very upset by the "secret" attack); • Very sensitive to ownership by a foreign government. • Summary: Would not consider the deal without extensive public discussion.

Exercise

1. As the Australian or Chinese side, propose some ways that this can become a Win/Win situation considering the real interests of both sides.
2. Now try to include some ideas that are *more than* Win/Win, ideas that increase the potential benefits to both sides, again considering the real interests of both sides.
3. Propose your ideas to your counterparts from the other country.

Section terminology

Probe: to explore and push for deeper, specific information

Section summary

> Learn what you and the other negotiators really want and try to satisfy those needs.

Principle-based negotiation

Principle-based negotiation is an approach described by Fisher, Ury and Patton (1991) in their book *Getting to Yes*. The approach proposes that all parties focus on principle (what they generally need and want), not on positions (specific points that can or cannot be given away).

Because specific positions are essentially Win/Lose, they result in imperfect negotiations and imperfect results. Compare the left side of Table 3.3 (positional, old-style thinking) to principle-based thinking. Fisher, Ury and Patton show us out-of-date thinking with only two choices, neither of which is suitable, see Table 3.3.

Fisher, Ury and Patton then show the way handle this Soft/Hard approach to negotiating, see Figure 3.4.

Fisher, Ury and Patton (1991) see a negotiation as a discussion about something important to those people and a chance to solve problems. This view is a positive starting point for progress. The opposite view (which we will avoid) is to see a negotiation only as a chance to get something. Also Fisher, Ury and Patton highlight two points that we have read about already:

* understanding the interests of the parties;
  * Interests include all sorts of things: money, reputation, future opportunities, relationships, respect, lowering risk, personal feelings, and so on.
* increasing the potential benefits beyond expectations at the start of negotiations.
  * Finding a new activity that increases the benefits to all parties: a new area of business, blocking a competitor, developing new resources, creating a new product and so on.

TABLE 3.3 Soft v. hard

Problem:
Bargaining based on positions: which approach?

Soft	Hard
Friends	Opponents
Seek agreement	Seek victory
Make concessions for relationship	Demand concessions in order to start relationship
Be soft on the problem and people	Be hard on the problem and people
Trust others	Distrust others
Change your position easily	Hold tight to your position
React to threats	Make threats
Disclose your bottom line	Lie about your bottom line
Accepted one-sided losses to reach agreement	Demand one-sided gains as the price of agreement
Search for answers they will accept	Search for your best and only answer
Insist on agreeing	Insist on your position
Avoid contests of will	Try to win contests of will
Give in to pressure	Apply pressure

Source: Fisher, Ury and Patton, 1991, p. 13

Change the approach entirely

Solution
Negotiate on the merits.
Principled
People are problem solvers.
Seek wise outcomes.
Separate people and problem.
Be soft on the people, hard on the problems.
Proceed with checks and balances, not emotional trust.
Put the focus on interests.
Discover all interests.
Create options for all sides to gain (mutual gains).
Use objective and fair standards.
Be open to reason, adjust to principles and fair thinking, not pressure.

FIGURE 3.4 From Hard v. Soft to Principled

Source: Fisher, Ury and Patton, 1991, p. 13

- Additionally, they tell us to:
  - o separate the people from the problem;
  - o focus on interests not positions;
  - o invent options for mutual gain;
  - o insist on using objective criteria.

Game theory

If you like thinking about game theory, you will enjoy this following discussion. You can see that Win/Lose and Win/Win negotiating are similar to the prisoner's dilemma game.

> Win/Lose negotiating is "imperfect" with poor results for one or all parties, but Win/Win negotiating is also not perfect. Why not? Write your ideas here.

_____

_____

Examine Table 3.4. Is "pretty good" the best we can hope for?

It is sometimes possible to improve "pretty good" through synergy and creating new value. Synergy opportunities allow negotiation parties to get new benefits together that they could not manage alone.

> If Win/Win is not perfect, is Win/Win with new value creation a better way? Is it perfect?

_____

_____

See http://money.howstuffworks.com/personal-finance/budgeting/negotiation5.htm for another explanation of this problem.

Thus you need to look for:

- common interests;
- mutual value creation;
- fair sharing of value creation;
- synergy.

TABLE 3.4 Value creation v. value sharing

	Low ← Value sharing →	High
High ↑ Value creation	Great for one party, but terrible for others	Pretty good for all parties
↓ **Low**	Terrible for all parties	Great for one party, but terrible for others

Synergy sounds nice, but what is it? Synergy (*syn* = together; *ergon* = work) means working together in a way that could not be done alone. Try to think of examples of possible synergy in negotiations that have been discussed previously in this text-book, such as the ChinAlco case.

_____

_____

_____

Section summary

Negotiate about key goals and principles; do not fight hard for specific posi-tions because these may lead to dead ends and limited value sharing.

4

STRUCTURE AND PLANNING

Building momentum

Building up speed toward success

Sometimes negotiations are successful because the parties develop confidence about dealing with each other. Even negotiators on the opposite sides of difficult issues can develop trust, confidence and empathy over time. Having successful agreements helps to build confidence among all parties. But how can you develop confidence the first time you negotiate a deal?

One way is to arrange the parts of the negotiation so that agreement can be reached on some easy parts early in the process. With early successes, all parties may feel more comfortable with difficult issues later. However, it could be a serious error to manage all the easy parts first: all your work could be lost if the last points in a negotiation cannot be resolved.

Disadvantages: Each part can cause all parts to fail.

Advantages: You can integrate issues and link them together. By the end, both sides are committed to agreeing, as "no-deal" becomes increasingly less appealing. However, be careful to avoid the error of being "in too deep" as previously discussed.

Another approach is to treat some or all issues separately. You might be satisfied to resolve some but not all of the issues.

Disadvantages: One side may walk away early leaving unresolved issues. Agreement on key issues may fail. All issues may not be integrated as well as possible.

Advantages: Each success creates good feeling and helps the entire project; Flexibility in adapting to the other parties.

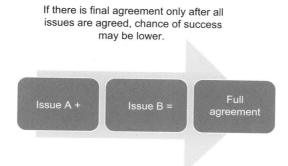

FIGURE 4.1 Strict ordering of issues

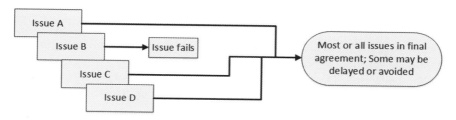

FIGURE 4.2 Flexible ordering of issues

To discuss with your partner – the best order

Easy issues first?	Helps build momentum, but the last items may be too tough, and the process may collapse. You may lose opportunities to integrate.
Easy things last?	You may resolve deepest problems early, but there is no chance to build momentum, confidence and successes in advance.
Your comments:	_____ _____

Is this the best way?

- Put some but not all the easy items in the beginning.
- Link some issues or groups of issues to allow good integrative negotiating.
- Even if you separate some issues, you should generally integrate issues where possible – do not allow all issues to become separate.
- Be flexible; choose the way most suited to that negotiation.
- Be flexible, unlink and relink issues if necessary.
- Agree to a rough approach (road map) with the other party.

Your comments: _____

_____

Useful hint: You can of course agree with your counterparts about the order in which to accomplish the negotiation tasks. Discussing the order and the reasons for it will help build the relationship.

Section summary

> Small successes can help build relationships and confidence. Also, after many successes and time, all sides may be less willing to give up and use their BATNA.

3D negotiation

Preplanning is a key teaching of this textbook. No person or team can manage a business negotiation without planning – lots of planning!

You know that 3D means three dimensions. The idea of 3D negotiation is for negotiators to think on three levels about any negotiation. The three dimensions are described in Table 4.1.

In which sequence should you execute the dimensions?

Start with: _____

Do next: _____

Last: _____

Tasks to be done in the setup phase

Determine the participants in the negotiation

Decide on the best team members for your side. Decide who will lead the team – an engineer, a sales and marketing person, a high level manager, or another person?

TABLE 4.1 Three dimensions of negotiation

Tactics	Deal design	Setup
At the table	On the drawing board	Away from the table
People and process	Value, substance and outcomes	Architecture
Build trust, handle hardball approaches, bridge intercultural gaps . . .	Create agreements that maximize value for both sides, improve on goals, are more sustainable . . .	Determine participants, BATNA, overall sequence, choices . . .

Source: Lax and Sebenius, 2006, p. 19

What skills and personalities do you want to have in your team? How many people should be on your team?

Be sure to consider the expectations of the other side as well as the issues in the negotiation as you make these decisions. At this point, a basic stakeholder analysis is necessary. List the key people and organizations and their main interests. Later, complete a more thorough analysis of all stakeholders and their interests. A thorough stakeholder analysis will be helpful for understanding the immediate surface issues as well as deeper issues. See Appendix VI for more on this.

In addition to your own personnel, you may be able to pick the people on the other sides that you will talk with. For example, you may want to approach a key figure in your organization in order to avoid a person with a bad reputation. You may prefer to deal with someone you already know, someone who is respected in the industry, someone with a reputation for negotiating well, a high ranking person, a very skilled engineer or other individuals for other reasons. In a very complex negotiation, you may want to have technical information presented by an expert individual or organization that is neutral to the negotiating parties in order to increase the knowledge of all parties. You may be able to include or exclude some organizations or individuals in advance by setting rules that other negotiation partners must agree to if they want to participate.

Determine your BATNA

Thoroughly investigate your alternatives to the negotiation. The stronger your BATNA, the more negotiating room and comfort you will have. As you investigate your BATNA, try to make it stronger. Even if making your BATNA stronger requires a lot of time, start the process.

Suppose that strengthening your BATNA will take more time than the planned length of your negotiation. Explain why it is a good idea to do it:

_____

_____

Determine the BATNAs of all parties

It is not enough to know your own BATNA. As discussed in the BATNA section, you will need to know the BATNA of the other side. Now is the time to learn about it and to weaken it. Why should you try (or not try) to weaken the BATNA of the other sides? _____

_____

_____

How might you be able to weaken the BATNA of another negotiation partner?

_____

_____

Overall sequence

During the early planning, you should check to see if there are any issues that must be resolved before other issues. For example, it might be necessary to determine a rough timeline before agreeing to milestones for portions of a project.

Your early planning and checking might identify some issues to be done in sequence; however, once the negotiation starts, it generally best not to stick to a rigid plan. A good negotiator reacts flexibly as new information appears.

Approximate timing and timescale of the negotiation

Consider the timing of the start and finish of the negotiation. Some points to include in the planning:

When:

- calendar year (major holidays or vacation periods to avoid);
- national holidays in your country and the countries of other negotiation partners;
- fiscal year (the very end of the fiscal year is usually extremely busy);
- business seasons (avoid times of year that are very busy for the other organizations).

How long:

- planning period on your side;
- estimated number of days, weeks, months, or years to talk;
- time constraints due to availability of resources;
- time expectations of the back table.

The back table

There is a hidden partner in almost every negotiation: the "back table". This refers to a boss, coworkers or another group that the negotiators will report to. Even the CEO reports to someone: the board! The back table (people or groups) is sometimes called a constituent group (Ware, 1980). The early phase of planning is the time to be sure that you and your back table are in close understanding about all expectations, limitations and issues related to the negotiation.

One of the limitations you must agree about with the back table is time. Often, people who are not part of the negotiation have the expectation that everything will be resolved quickly. The truth, however, is often very different. In fact, the higher the quality of communication in the negotiations, the more likely that questions will arise requiring more research time. Good negotiation usually means good solutions. Good solutions, of course, require time to develop. The lesson is clear: you will need lots of time, maybe more than your peers and bosses expect. Be sure to change their expectations.

See Chapter 8 for more discussion about the back table.

Research to do list

Develop a list steps for your research and a list specific things to learn about. Your research to-do list will increase in size as you go on. But the list should start by fulfilling the phrase, "Know the facts, know the people." View the video of Dr. Kurt Biedenkopf at http://bit.ly/1riIzdN for comments from this experienced negotiator. If the link does not work, visit the YouTube channel for "The Negotiation Challenge" and look for the video titled "Kurt Biedenkopf on negotiations" there. His summary in the first 25 seconds packs tremendous insight and power.

This simple phrase, "know the facts, know the people," is a directive to learn in detail about the negotiation issues and the people and organizations related to them. This means knowing something about the personalities of the negotiators on the other teams. It may be possible to learn about them in advance, as well as to learn about them through interactions during the negotiations.

As for the facts, it is up to you to search every possible source, online or not, for relevant facts and information. Sources you might include:

- recent newspaper articles;
- old newspaper archives;
- specialist industry periodicals;
- court records;
- network of business acquaintances, friends and family;
- government contracts;
- and so on.

Checklist

Develop a checklist of the basics that you need to achieve during negotiation. See the next section for more information.

Section summary

> Most of the work in negotiating happens before the negotiation. Use multiple planning methods to prepare.

Basic planning

> When preparing for a negotiation you need to prepare your negotiation shopping list. This is a list of the things you want to get out of the negotiation.
> *Bare Knuckle Negotiating*, Hazeldine, p. 35

Prepare a list of what you want to get from your current negotiation.

_____

_____

_____

The simplest form of planning is the shopping list previously mentioned, a checklist of things you reasonably hope to accomplish. A checklist is a good starting point, but we can expand a checklist easily to make it more useful.

First, make a list of results that you have to get. These necessary items are ones that you must accomplish if the negotiation is to be better than your BATNA. Second, list the results that you would like to get additionally but that are not absolutely necessary. Third, list the things that you can reasonably trade away in order to get what you must have and want. Use these three categories to create a HIT list (LaFond, Vine and Welch, 2010):

H – Have to get

I – Intend to get

T – Trade in order to get H and I items

Read this short case and create a HIT list for the things you need.

Case: The right hotel, the right deal

You are seeking a large hotel to host a convention in Singapore. There are many hotels and the convention will start year after next, so you have much time and several choices. Before you talk to the hotel you prefer most, you must think about your needs.

You expect to have about 1,000 attendees over three days. The hotel has only 290 rooms, so you hope to reserve all or most of them for your attendees until a little before the event. It would be best to block them until two weeks before the event, but really the attendees should plan and reserve four to eight weeks in advance. The retail cost of a hotel room is $250 (about 2000 HKD), and this is certainly too expensive for most of your attendees, so you feel it is necessary to lower the price to at most $190 per night. You could guarantee some of those rooms will be filled, but you are nervous about guaranteeing all of them, of course. Breakfasts at the hotel are quite expensive in addition to the hotel room, so you would like to secure free breakfasts for your ten staff members and a 20–50 percent discount for all conference attendees. You know that the hotel usually offers free access to the swimming pool, but you have heard the pool is small and crowded, so it might not really be useful for your attendees. The fitness room, however, is supposed to be quite good but is not free.

Now consider the items you need to get, would like to get and could trade. List them appropriately in Table 4.2.

Use Table 4.2 for your HIT list.

TABLE 4.2 HIT list

Have to get		Intend to get	Tradable

★ Note that "have to get" includes "have to get rid of"

TABLE 4.3 Expanded HIT list with steps

Have to get	Steps
Price at or below $200/night	Start by asking for $145; accept $155 if free wireless; accept $175 if free wireless and gym, pool and 50 percent breakfast discount; accept $190–$200 if the hotel has all of the above and additional suitable services to offer.

The HIT list in Table 4.2 is easy to manage and useful, but it is only a starting point. We can improve on it. One of the improvements will be adding steps between your starting point and your acceptable minimum reserve point.

The expanded HIT list, Table 4.3, is a simplified version of the Raiffa scorecard discussed later in this chapter. The Raiffa scorecard is more powerful and useful, but first we will discuss backward mapping as a way to structure and plan the negotiation.

Identifying interests

In this section, we will go much deeper into the process of negotiation planning. Understanding the interests of the parties is a vital step in planning. Your notes should include your interests and what you guess or know about the other parties' interests and goals.

   . . . what are valid interests to include?
   . . . all sides (you and *them*)

Please choose some interests that could be included in your notes:

__ your time restrictions	__ their time restrictions
__ your maximum price	__ their minimum price
__ your most and least important issues	__ relationships among their negotiators
__ your long-term hopes	__ recent trend of their stock price
__ your _____	__ their priorities

How to determine interests

Do not take your boss's list of preferred outcomes as the final list of your own interests – investigate all interests of all parties thoroughly. Most business negotiations involve money, but there may be many more issues and interests. Start with the ones in the interest grid in Table 4.4 and add to the categories.

To dig deeper into interests, Lax and Sebenius suggest these steps in *3D Negotiation* (2006, p. 76):

> Four practices that help you get interests right:
> 1. ask, listen, probe;
> 2. use public sources to map interests;
> 3. get insight from internal sources;
> 4. get insight from knowledgeable advisers.

We have already discussed the first one, asking and listening. The third one we can understand as asking people you know in your network or in your company who might have some insight or information about the other party. The fourth one we can understand as asking professionals and consultants beyond your coworkers. Let's consider the second one: public sources.

Public sources means looking widely at newspaper articles, special industry journals, newsletters, internet chat rooms, speeches, YouTube videos, books, blogs, comments by experts, SEC filings, tax information and all other sources that are legally and publicly available.

Note that it is also possible to get information through unethical methods: misrepresenting yourself to people familiar with the other parties and the planning, stealing data, paying another person to steal data, etc. None of these methods are acceptable in the real world of business. These methods will damage or destroy

TABLE 4.4 Simplified interest grid

Interest Category	Our understanding of this issue	Their understanding of this issue
Financial		
Reputational		
Personal		
Staffing		
Capacity		
Business cycle		
Regulatory		
Timing		

business relationships with negotiating partners and others when discovered. Moreover, they may result in legal troubles.

Exercise: Discuss with your partners how you will use public sources to learn about interests for the final team negotiation. Write down some sources and what you expect to find in them:

a. _____

b. _____

c. _____

d. _____

e. _____

Generally, you should consider all possible interests when planning for the negotiation. In the end, you should try to make a final list with notes. You can carry a list like this to the negotiating table with you. See Appendix III for a planning sheet based on Brett's planning document.

Backward mapping

In their book *3D Negotiation*, Lax and Sebenius (2006) suggest "mapping backward" as a process for crafting the agreement and the negotiating strategy. First, determine what your final agreement should look like. Next, go backward toward the starting point by understanding the barriers to agreeing. As you identify and understand each barrier to the agreement, you can prepare positions and offers that will make a final agreement possible.

Deal breakers

The processes of investigation, research, planning, and especially backward planning, should help you identify problems that are so difficult that they cannot be overcome. These may be deal breakers. It is important to identify possible deal breakers and confirm whether or not they are unresolvable early in the process of the negotiation. If the deal breakers cannot be resolved, they will stop the negotiation.

TABLE 4.5 Brett's negotiation planning document

Issue	Self			Other	
Investment	Position: $3.5 mil			Position: possibly $2–4 mil	
	Priority Very high	timing-ASAP		Priority High	ROI; timing of payment

Source: Brett, 2007.

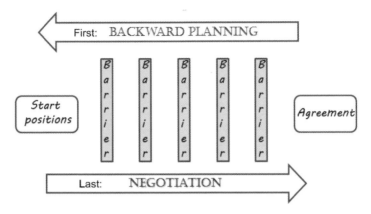

Work backward from the targeted agreement when planning

FIGURE 4.3 Backward planning

Leaving them until the end of the talks will result in the complete loss of time and effort invested.

Deal breakers often are items that one side requires with no options for adjusting or avoiding. In the Chinalco and Rio Tinto case described in the previous chapter, 18 percent ownership by a foreign company was a deal breaker in the eyes of one stakeholder, the Australian government.

Game theory

> Consider your expectations as you develop the deal you want. Howard Raiffa (2002) writes that even experienced negotiators generally expect better results than they really get. Therefore, be sure that the deal you want is really acceptable to the counterparty.

You may recognize this backward mapping approach from game theory: backward induction. Game theory shows how powerful a tool this is for choosing the right path to the outcome you want. The process is the same: identify the possible outcomes; select the best one you can reasonably attain; and understand the steps necessary to reach that outcome by working backward through the interests, needs and positions of the other parties.

In the process of mapping backwards, points in the deal you want must not appear in either the unacceptable to the other side or the not agreeing sections. Compare these carefully to see if there are conflicts you must resolve before the negotiations start. You can find blanks prepared for backward mapping in Appendix III.

Appendix III contains various planning documents. Use all of them or only the ones you feel comfortable with.

Now consider the next negotiation in this class. Please consider the final goal of your side and your counterparts. Draw a full-page map approximately following backward mapping from Lax and Sebenius.

Section summary

> Backward mapping is a good tool for planning. To use this or any other planning tool, you must know the interests of all the parties in the negotiation.

Priority and outcome mapping

It can be confusing to track all issues and the possible outcomes. Howard Raiffa (2002), in his book *Negotiation Analysis: The Art and Science of Negotiating*, offers a practical way to manage priorities and possible outcomes. He suggests Table 4.6 to organize interests and outcomes, and he suggests using points that add up to 100 to evaluate importance of issues and the benefits of the outcomes.

A blank scorecard can be found in Appendix VIII of this booklet.

TABLE 4.6 Sample Raiffa scorecard

Issue	Issue value	Outcome	Outcome value
1 Cost	15	a. over $15 mil	15
		b. $15 mil	12
		c. $10 mill (reserve)	7
2 investment	10	a. $3 mil and shared staff input	10
		b. $3 mil	7
		c. $1 mil	4
		d. none (reserve)	0
3 intangible property	20	a. retain all with full control	20
		b. retain key portions	17
		c. retain less important items	15
		d. sell all (reserve)	10
4 joint development	30	a. projects Alpha, Beta, and Gamma	30
		b. only project Alpha	15
5 joint access to staff	25	a. share IT and R&D staff and skills	25
		b. share IT staff and skills	20
		c. share administrative tasks and skills	10
		d. none	2
Total=100 maximum	100	Total of selected outcomes	

Source: Raiffa, 2002, p. 217

How to make and manage a Raiffa scorecard

This scorecard is a helpful way to simplify the issues in a negotiation and easily understand the choices you might pursue or trade.

Step 1: write down the key issues;

Step 2: weigh the issues by importance with points adding up to 100;

Step 3: write down alternative possible outcomes for each issue;

Step 4: set points for each possible outcome, up to the maximum for that issue;

Step 5: consider all the points, you can now see priorities and preferences – use this information to structure your negotiation and decide what you can trade or abandon in order to get something more valuable.

Step 6: As you negotiate, track the outcomes that you agree to. Of course, you must remain flexible and adjust to new value possibilities that you may discover during the negotiation.

Practice: Fill out the scorecard in Table 4.7 for one of the cases in this course.

Evaluating success

The Raiffa scorecard can also help evaluate success. After a complex negotiation, it is often difficult to know if you did well or not so well. A glance at the scorecard in Table 4.8 would show quickly the overall results. The shaded lines in Table 4.8 are the agreed outcomes, so we can see that the negotiators got 66 out of 100 points for getting 1b, 2c, 3d, 4b and 5a.

Maybe they should have provided better reasoning for issues 3 and 4! On the other hand, they were successful with 5d, and that was a very important issue and the best outcome. Perhaps if Project Alpha goes well, they can renegotiate in order to extend the agreement to include Beta and Gamma.

TABLE 4.7 Blank Raiffa scorecard

Issue	Issue value	Outcome	Outcome value
Total=100 maximum	100	Total of selected outcomes	

TABLE 4.8 Sample Raiffa scorecard for evaluating results

Issue	Issue value	Outcome	Outcome value
1 Cost	15	a. over $15 mil	15
		b. $15 mil	12
		c. $10 mill (reserve)	7
2 investment	10	a. $3 mil and shared staff input	10
		b. $3 mil	7
		c. $1 mil	4
		d. none (reserve)	0
3 intangible property	20	a. retain all with full control	20
		b. retain key portions	17
		c. retain less important items	15
		d. sell all (reserve)	10
4 joint development	30	a. projects Alpha, Beta and Gamma	30
		b. only project Alpha	15
5 joint access to staff	25	a. share IT and R&D staff and skills	25
		b. share IT staff and skills	20
		c. share administrative tasks and skills	10
		d. none	2
Total=100 maximum	100	Total of selected outcomes	66

Section summary

> Outcome mapping is a good tool for planning. To use this or any other planning tool, you must know the interests of all the parties in the negotiation.

The sequence of talk at the table

After considering the setup and planning that must occur before talks start, we still need to understand the best sequence of events at the table. What to discuss first? Is there anything that should be done early on? Or avoided?

Consider the following elements of negotiation. Write a number before each one to indicate what should come first, second, third, and so on.

___ Major issues, get to the point   ___ Small talk
___ Company history   ___ Rules and protocol
___ Problem solving   ___ Agenda
___ Information sharing   ___ Introductions and personal experience

Please write your reason for the item that you chose as #1. _____

_____

_____

Let's consider the pros and cons of starting with each point.

- Agenda: Agreeing to the agenda is an important process that may be quite complicated. Each party may have reasons for starting with certain issues. Because it is complex, and possibly divisive, it is better not to start with this.
- Company history: Each company has its own history that helps define what it is and how it works. This information is important to understanding interests and motivation. However, it may be useful to first understand the people.
- Information sharing: The process and degree of information sharing develop with interaction. It cannot be pushed into a first activity at a first meeting. It should instead occur over many meetings.
- Introductions and personal experience: This activity is a good way to start any meeting, especially when participants are new to each other. This activity and small talk can mix easily together. Some individuals and cultures will make this longer or shorter based, for example, on preference, rank and comfort level.
- Major issues, get to the point: It is best not to start here, as parties are likely to come directly to a conflict or deadlock. It is important to first understand people, interests, organizations and details in order to solve possible problems.
- Problem solving: This activity requires time and much information. It cannot be completed successfully in a first meeting.
- Rules and protocol: This topic is important to establish early in the relationship in order to avoid unintended false steps, insults and bruised egos. Usually this is best placed after introductions and small talk.
- Small talk: A good way to start any meeting. It helps to create a positive atmosphere and starts the flow of information sharing. Some individuals and cultures will prefer more or less small talk. Prepare accordingly with suitable casual topics.

Section summary

> Start face-to-face interactions with introductions and possibly gift exchanges and small talk. Use these interactions to build rapport and to start the flow of information.

5
SOME CULTURAL CONSIDERATIONS

Top-down/bottom-up

Please read about the two approaches in Table 5.1 – which feels most comfortable to you?

TABLE 5.1 Top–down, bottom–up

Top-down	Bottom-up
This means getting the global "large picture" goals in order before dealing with details and specific issues. As the overall picture becomes clear, the logical path to achieving it also becomes clear.	This means dealing with specifics before coming to a global conclusion. As the specifics are discussed and agreed, they build the larger, final picture.
Example: generally including or excluding some areas of activity before working out details.	Example: negotiating the details of an agreement (order volume, delivery time, unit price, services, etc.) before coming to broader issues.

Does it start from an agreement on general principles and proceed to specific items (top-down) or does it begin with an agreement on specifics, such as price, delivery date and product quality, the sum total of which becomes the contract (bottom-up)?
Source: Salacuse, 2004

Neither approach is perfect or "correct". Be flexible and work with your counterparts and team members to view negotiations from both perspectives. Your counterparts may not even realize that they like to progress top–down or bottom–up.

Design your negotiation approach(es) in advance. A good negotiator learns to design the negotiation before starting the actual negotiation meetings. Before means long before, because time is necessary to consider, learn and redesign. If you can, agree with the other party in advance about which approach to use in order to avoid misunderstandings.

Top-down, bottom-up and culture

> This dimension [top down / bottom up] captures whether negotiators build agreement by negotiating specifics, such as product characteristics, price, and terms of delivery, or whether they start from general principles and then proceed to specific items.
>
> (Salacuse, 2003, p. 338)

> Finnish respondents strongly preferred a top down approach, with 85% positioned on that end of the continuum (. . .). Indian responses stood in sharp contrast with more than 50% preferring a bottom-up approach, although once again a sizeable portion (27%) located at the top-down end. The Turkish response pattern leaned toward a top down approach, while Mexican and US patterns reflected no strong preference.
>
> (Metcalf et al., 2006, p. 388)

Cultural issues: If possible, establish the mutual starting point (top or bottom) before you arrive at the negotiating table. In the real world, you may come to know what to expect from certain people, companies or within a country or region. Do people from the western part of your country prefer to start top-down while people from the eastern part of your country prefer to start bottom-up? What about people from different parts of China? Or Australia? What about companies? Does Mitsubishi (Japan) work top-down? Does SingTech (Singapore) work bottom-up? Always try to check first by talking to the other side or talking to people with experience.

As previously mentioned, expectations may vary from country to country or company to company. Metcalf et al. (2006) have this to say:

- build momentum with Indians by negotiating agreement on smaller issues;
- build rapport with Finns by laying out the general themes and principles behind the negotiations.

Note: Metcalf et al. make it clear that not all Finns, Indians, Mexicans, etc. react or think the same way. Never stereotype regarding country and culture! Be flexible and react to the clues you learn about your counterparties as you research and as you talk to them. Check about the individuals in advance if possible. If you cannot check in advance, discover their preferred approaches at the first encounter.

Review

Which is better, top-down or bottom-up? Neither one is objectively better. However, it is generally a good idea first to explore some global issues (top-down) before getting into details (bottom-up). You might start by generally agreeing on the overall goal, then turn to groups of issues or individual issues.

In your planning phase, long before you talk, you must consider top-down, global issues. If you know the global picture, you may be able to more successfully link details and integrate issues.

Your comments:

_____

_____

Section summary

Before the negotiations, plan starting with the big picture (top-down) and again starting with the details (bottom-up). Adapt flexibly to the approach the other side uses.

Culture and negotiation

In the previous section, we learned from Salacuse and Metcalf et al. that negotiators from some countries have preferences in how they negotiate. What preferences do people in your country or region have for negotiating?

_____

_____

Interview: Ask three people in this class all of the following questions, noting their home country or region. When you answer other students, avoid answers like "both".

Which do you think is more important for a successful negotiation team?

Highly skilled members (e.g. engineers)		High level figure as a member (e.g. CEO)
	1	
	2	
	3	

Should a negotiator represent an organization or his/her own self?

Only self – show your quality as a negotiator		Only the organization – your prestige has no importance
	1	
	2	
	3	

Which is better for you?

It is good to mix all the issues together and get all the opinions at once.		It is much easier and less confusing to handle issues one by one.
	1	
	2	
	3	

How do you prefer business negotiations to proceed – casually or quite formally?

Casual is best – we can discuss in conference rooms or at dinner, no one should feel pressure about position and roles.		Formal arrangements are best – we can easily know when we are "talking business" or relaxing and know other persons' roles.
	1	
	2	
	3	

How do you prefer business negotiations to proceed – quickly or at a slower speed?

Fast is best – we should come to a conclusion quickly in order to decrease the cost of negotiation and so we can get on to other business.		Slower is best – we should use time to learn about the projects and opportunities.
	1	
	2	
	3	

What do you think is the point of negotiation?

The overall purpose is to discuss business issues.		The point is to complete a suitable deal.
	1	
	2	
	3	

Which idea about contracts feels best to you?

A contract is a fixed document that you must follow exactly.		A contract is a starting point for immediate and future business.
	1	
	2	
	3	

Questions developed based on concepts from Trompenaars and Hampden-Turner (1998) and Hofstede and Hofstede (2005).

The previously mentioned questions are not easy because the answers are limited and you may not propose your own ideas. The questions and answers are designed to help you understand that people might think in ways that are very different, approaching the same problem from different directions. Knowing that approaches might be very different helps you adjust constructively instead of being surprised and upset.

Expectations

Culture is deeply connected to, even defined by, people's expectations of each other. With experience, a negotiator from one cultural background can learn the expectations of another cultural group. With that knowledge, the negotiator can adjust behavior to come closer to the expectations of the other side. A 2013 interview with an American business negotiator showed that Japanese business people, in his experience, were more formal than Americans, and he adjusted his behavior appropriately for them.

> Interviewer: How do you usually, ehm, how do you usually address your [Japanese] negotiating counterpart?
> Very formally or informally?
> Interviewee: Yes, yes, very formally. To me it just comes naturally that you need to be formal.
> Interviewer: mhmm, what about the Americans?
> Interviewee: They don't give a flip, haha.
> *Negotiations between Japan and the United States,*
> Sepstrup and Ipsen, p. 76

The negotiator in the example expects to behave more formally with Japanese businesspeople because of his ideas about Japan and his experience there. However, Japanese businesspeople might be even more formal with each other or with other East Asians than with Americans. Japanese businesspeople generally consider Americans to be more casual, and they prepare themselves to act accordingly toward Americans. The difference this author has seen in various encounters involving North Americans and Japanese is striking: in meetings, Japanese individuals may smoothly transition between friendly smiles and handshakes for North Americans, and formal bows and strict greeting formulas appropriate to the relative age and rank of other Japanese businesspeople.

The example from Sepstrup and Ipsen shows Americans adjusting to their ideas about Japanese people and Japanese people adjusting to their ideas about Americans. It seems that all sides in intercultural encounters often mutually adjust to the behaviors they think the others prefer.

In the end, expectations, cultural behaviors and actions of real people in real situations are very fluid.

> Consider a country or region that you know well. What kind of negotiation behavior can you expect in that country? Would it be the same in the east and west? North and south?

> What kind of behavior can you expect from an individual, maybe someone named Paul Tomlinson, from San Francisco, California, US?

> Write your very brief conclusion about culture and negotiation:

Culture and stereotyping – not a reliable approach

> . . . individuals and groups within cultures may be united on some dimensions (Indians on direct communication), deeply divided or split on others (Indians on attitudes), and uncommitted on others (Finns on risk-taking). It is no longer acceptable nor is it accurate or useful – if it ever was – for, say, an American negotiator to expect a Mexican counterpart to be relationship-oriented or an American compatriot to be contract-oriented. Our findings point to the inherent inaccuracy of what Osland and Bird (2000) have referred to as "sophisticated stereotyping."
>
> (Metcalf et al., 2006, p. 393)

Short version

People from one country may have some similarities, or maybe not. You can learn about general styles and cultural preferences from regional business guidebooks.

These guidebooks can help you learn practical information about gifts, general behaviors and values. But you cannot safely apply that general information to individuals. Do not stereotype!

What to do: Learn about the individuals and their companies in addition to learning the general behaviors of the appropriate cultural groups.

Culture and language

When you are negotiating with a group from another country with a different language, you will probably interact in English. In this situation, is it a good idea for you to speak in your own native language with your negotiation team? Y   N

Please explain your answer:

_____

_____

Browaeys and Price (2011) in their textbook *Understanding Cross-Cultural Management* compare cultural approaches to common management issues. They compare five areas of management: planning, organizing, staffing, directing and controlling to eight dimensions of culture. The dimensions are relative scales of how strongly a culture may prefer behaviors. The relative positions of a person, a group or company on the dimensions highlights areas where people may work well together or not, in part because their expectations are met or not.

The eight dimensions of culture they discuss include:

- high versus low-context;
- doing versus being;
- polychronic versus monochromic;
- future versus past orientation;
- hierarchic versus equality;
- public versus private;
- collectivist versus individualistic;
- competitive versus cooperative.

Mapping one's own expectations to those of teammates or counterparties may show how you can cooperate or where you might conflict. If conflict is on the horizon, planning and learning and adjusting may help to avoid the conflict or even create opportunities to craft a new and mutually agreeable approach. A comparison of cultures might look like Figure 5.1 from Browaeys and Price (2011, p. 137).

In Figure 5.1, we can see large differences between ideas about time scheduling (polychronic), competitiveness, individualism, hierarchy and public space. On the other hand, both sides may have similar ideas about future planning. With these points in mind, the sides can prepare to learn about the differences in detail, looking for ways that they can complement each other or resolve conflicts. Even

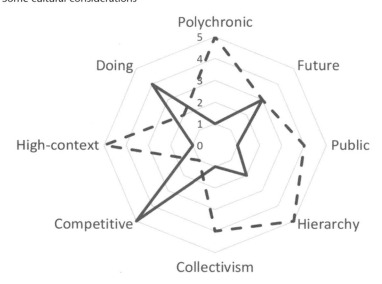

FIGURE 5.1 Profile comparing two cultures

if only one side conducts this kind of cultural mapping and comparison, they can prepare appropriately and communicate their findings and concerns to the other parties.

In the end, negotiations across cultures may be more time consuming than comparable negotiations within the same culture. Brett and Okumura (1998) showed that mutual gains were significantly lower when negotiating teams were from different cultural backgrounds.

See Appendix V for more insights on culture and negotiating.

Corporate culture

You must also learn about the culture and beliefs of the businesses you will interact with. Some business sectors have a corporate culture that sets them apart from other areas. For example, the world of IT is known for late nights, flexible hours, casual clothing and working intensively as projects come to a head. On the other hand, the world of banking is better known for regular hours, working at a reasonable pace and sticking closely to the rules of banking imposed by government or international standards.

However, inside a business sector, not all the organizations and companies may share a culture. For example, within Japan's finance sector, Mitsui Sumitomo Bank and MUFJ have very different corporate cultures with different levels of power and

TABLE 5.2 Corporate culture comparison

Samsung	Lucky Gold
Emphasizes individual merit and personal skills over the team. The person is number one.	Emphasizes team success over individual ability. Harmony is number one.
Empowers individuals to work fast.	Requires individuals to work within the system and company hierarchy.
Large portion of pay is based on personal performance (bonus).	Personal bonuses are not usual.
Product development and marketing are highly integrated.	Product development and marketing are more independent.

flexibility given to workers. In Korea, Samsung and Lucky Gold have very different cultures, despite being in the same industry.

Section summary

> Be aware of cultural preferences and behaviors in teams from other regions or countries, but never expect specific behavior – always be flexible and sensitive towards your counterparties.

Weak/strong points of North American negotiators

Understanding some common failings or strong points among a group of people might help you avoid communication errors, deadlock and failed negotiations. In addition to gaining some insight into another group, Tables 5.3 and 5.4 may help describe yourself and your coworkers and counterparties within your culture. After reading about the cultures broadly described, try listing some strong and weak points of your cultural background with appropriate comments that will help you and others work together.

Broadly, it is possible to list some common strengths and weaknesses of negotiators from a culture. But do not apply this data to all people from those places! That sort of stereotyping will most likely lead a negotiator into errors. However, it is possible to set your general expectations using this data. The next step is to compare your expectations to the reality of the people you interact with to determine if they are as described in Tables 5.3 and 5.4 or as described in other sources. You can only cautiously apply the ideas about weaknesses and strengths once you understand the people involved. As discussed elsewhere in this textbook, know the people, know the facts!

TABLE 5.3 Awareness: some weak points of North American negotiators

Typical weak points	Advice for North American negotiators
Impatience	• Increase travel time and travel flexibility – deals outside of North America often require significantly more time for interruptions, relationship building and back table negotiations. • Let the other sides know you are not under time pressure and can continue the discussion remotely or on another visit. • Propose that the finalizing meetings be held in North America to decrease the time pressure on your side. • Train your boss – if your organization is not aware of the extensive time commitment necessary in many cases, you will have to train key staff regarding reasonable expectations.
Outcome over process	• Use the negotiation process to build the relationship and create new opportunities. • Laser focus on a single driving deal or issue is not appreciated in much of the world, although it is appreciated in some places.
Poor sensitivity regarding relationships	• Learn to identify key parties, including those not directly involved in the negotiation. Be aware that a government agency or senior industry partner may be standing in the wings with significant power over decisions. • Identify patterns in context that reveal background information. This is sometimes called high or low context. Low context cultures need all details spelled out explicitly; high context cultures quickly see relationships that seem invisible to others. • North America is usually rated middle/low context. People from this background may be uncomfortable with the bluntness of North Europeans and the indirect communications of East Asians.
Profit over process	• Learn to accept lower profit if it means making your supplier/ partner stronger and more valuable in the long term.
Overuse of remote media	• Your partners may not appreciate the low cost and speed of telephone, email, videoconference and other media. Face-to-face work may be necessary, at least until the relationship has developed.
Short term thinking	• Trapped by budgets and quarterly reports, North American negotiators may feel they have to agree and move on. • Train your organization to expect delayed paydays in comparison to dealing with local organizations.
Detail orientation in contracts	• North Americans tend to place great value on detail in negotiations and contracts. Some parts of the world may view this as wasteful and indicative of an untrustworthy partner. • It may be necessary to let some details go entirely, or move them from the main document to addenda and follow-up documents.
Contract is written in stone	• Countries with strict legal systems tend to see contracts as fixed documents with little room for interpretation. Other parts of the world expect the contract to serve as a starting point for serious details and discussions. • It may be necessary to accept a "loose contract" as a first step to concrete work and as an invitation to work out specifics.
Face	• Most North Americans are sensitive to their own loss of face, but not to protecting the face or building up the face of others. North Americans should try to learn how to better manage face in negotiations.

Source: Used with permission from the Athabasca University Faculty of Business.

TABLE 5.4 Awareness: some strong points of North American negotiators

Typical strong points	Comments on North American negotiators
Agility	• North American organizations, especially for-profit businesses, tend to have quick decision making. They can change approaches and accept new ideas speedily. This helps them adjust to changing business environments, technologies and partners.
Speed	• North American businesses tend to deliver products quickly with short turnaround time, and often with the willingness and ability to assign additional resources.
Attitude	• A healthy can-do attitude often helps overcome social and political barriers that may seem impossibly difficult in more traditional societies.
Moderately affective	• Affective refers to the degree to which emotions are expressed. North Americans tend to be in the middle of the scale, neither extremely poker-faced nor extremely expressive. This allows them some ability to react appropriately to more or less affective counterparts.
	• Research in advance about what is appropriate and expected will benefit the negotiator.
Contract writing	• Detailed contracts seem to be a hallmark of litigious North American thinking. The potential benefit is that proper management of contingencies written in the contract can benefit both sides if explained and developed satisfactorily to both sides.

Source: Used with permission from the Athabasca University Faculty of Business.

Section summary

> North American negotiators generally are direct and result oriented. They are usually meticulous about contract contents. Adjust carefully to the style of the North American individuals and groups you work with.

Weak/strong points of Japanese negotiators

Common behaviors

It is also wise to look for current behaviors and expectations among negotiators from a certain culture. Research done during the writing of this textbook by the authors shows that a large percentage (77 percent) of experienced business negotiators in Japan rarely or never experience haggling with other Japanese negotiators. Therefore, you might want to avoid haggling in order not to disturb a positive relationship. Other findings regarding Japanese-Japanese business negotiations (data gathered in 2013 and 2014):

- large teams are common, i.e. four or more members (87 percent);
- common to develop new value during the negotiations (80 percent);

TABLE 5.5 Awareness: some weak points of Japanese negotiators

Typical weak points	Advice for Japanese negotiators
Excessively patient	• Other parties may misunderstand patience as a failure to understand the proposals or external pressures such as time limitations. Be sure to exhibit active listening in a way that your counterparties can understand. It is best to show your listening skills by frequently summarizing and paraphrasing.
Poor communicators	• Build up communication skills not only in speaking but also in graphical representation. Learn to collaboratively develop a joint image of a project.
Develop trust slowly	• Learn to share information and give information at a similar rate and scale to information received from other parties.
Slow decision making	• Accelerate internal team communication, communication with the back table and decentralize decision making. • Learn to quickly consider and offer ideas without taking time for detailed development.
Bound to Japanese business calendar	• Clarify to other parties those periods (e.g. the end of the fiscal year) when you cannot work on the negotiation.
Prefer detailed resolution of plans and outcomes in high detail (bottom–up)	• Consider proposals at a general level without detailed analysis of all inputs and outcomes. Complex proposals can be broken into chunks that can be accepted or rejected without detailing all issues.
Formal processes	• Often Japanese teams prefer formal processes such as using a junior team member as spokesperson, setting seating arrangements and so on. These steps may be comforting to the Japanese side, but alienating or confusing for counterparties.
Intransigence	• When rejecting a proposal, explain why it is being rejected, how it could be made acceptable and alternatives that correct the problem. • Negotiators from other cultures may not know when the Japanese side is embarrassed or concerned about protecting face. Explain to those counterparties how to help save face.
Major decisions not made at the table	• Major decisions are often not made by the negotiators, but by corporate headquarters (back table). Work to make this process move quickly with frequent communications and well-designed recommendations to the back table. One experienced Japanese negotiator explained that he brought his boss to the negotiation table physically when the deal was very close to complete (last meeting) in order to speed the closing steps.

TABLE 5.6 Awareness: some strong points of Japanese negotiators

Typical strong points	Comments on Japanese negotiators
Patient	• A benefit to all parties – however, counterparties may not know the Japanese parties are patient because of poor use of active listening skills appropriate for the other language and culture.
Long term thinking	• Let the other side know early in the process about the timescale regarding agreement terms, ROI, breakeven, renegotiation, etc.
Prefer detailed resolution of plans and outcomes in high detail (bottom-up)	• The final result of preference for high detail is a well designed product or process. The time required, however, may harm the negotiation process. Learn to move quickly through details.
Good at understanding relationships to stakeholders	• Let the other side know that you are considering how they interact with their shareholders. In some cases, you may understand their relationships better than they do!
Very closely synchronized with the back table	• This close synchronization and understanding saves time and trouble for all parties. However, the counterparties may not understand that major decisions will not be made by the negotiation team, but at headquarters. Be sure to make the process move quickly.
Willing to take time for site visits, research and preparation	• Increases understanding of the aspects of a complex negotiation. Cost and time are not considered "wasted".
Insightful	• Japanese teams tend to be good at whole-picture intuitive thinking, but it does not happen quickly – intuition does not come in leaps, but rather it comes in small, steady steps.

- positive emotions are clearly demonstrated (82 percent);
- progress is often made outside of the normal, formal work environment (62 percent);
- indirect logic, rather than direct logic, is normal (100 percent);
- often a rush to complete before the end of the fiscal year (61 percent);
- threats are rarely or never made (100 percent);
- great care is given to the seating of the participants based on their relative rank (90 percent).

Part of your preparation before dealing with people from another culture should be to look for information similar to the previous points by reading, talking to experienced people and communicating with people from the other culture.

Section summary

> Japanese negotiators may be indirect in communication, seeking to understand layers of issues before coming to specifics. They are often highly patient in negotiation and well informed about issues. Adjust carefully to the style of the Japanese individuals and groups you work with.

Weak/strong points of Chinese negotiators

Section summary

> Chinese negotiators tend to value exchanges of favors, which are flexible acts of mutual benefit and lead to relationship building and flexibility in negotiation. Exchanging information may not lead to good relationships. Adjust carefully to the style of the Chinese individuals and groups you work with.

TABLE 5.7 Awareness: some weak points of Chinese negotiators

Typical weak points	Advice for Chinese negotiators
Prefer to conform to existing conventions	• Show your foreign partners how other organizations conform to conventions and how this will benefit them. • However, as non–Chinese partners become increasingly sensitive to price, prepare to allow some flexibility regarding wage rates, other costs and procedures.
Overinvesting in amicable relationships	• Chinese teams may sometimes rate relationship as more important than pursuing value. They must be careful not to exchange too much value for relationships – the strongest relationships are based on mutual problem solving.
Disputes resolved informally	• Complex disputes may arise or the partners, especially foreign partners, may not be able to participate in creating solutions. Therefore, Chinese organizations should include mutually agreeable language in the initial agreement to help resolve disagreements
Very dependent on a superior figure	• Chinese teams generally feel they have to obey their superior staff – even if that person makes a snap decision. • To counteract this, Chinese teams should agree in advance that major decisions will not be made without consultation within the team that includes input from specialists.
Paying insufficient attention to detailed and specialized contract clauses	• Negotiating teams, especially in state owned enterprises, may have different staff than the executing team, giving rise to problems that are difficult to solve. Negotiation teams should include key staff members who will execute the work, not only business and sales specialists.

Typical weak points	Advice for Chinese negotiators
Time pressure in complex negotiations	• Chinese organizations are not immune to time pressure, especially where negotiations are complex and have taken a long time. Time pressure may not be seen so much as a rush to complete an agreement as much as in a rush to approve it. Therefore, neither the negotiation team nor top management should hurry the governance of contracts.
One-sided information sharing	• Non-Chinese teams, especially from Europe and North America, build relationships through sharing information. The Chinese team should share its information and insights, not limit itself to gathering information only.
Face saving	• Foreign teams may not be sensitive to face-saving issues, such as the exact decision-making power of a negotiator or personalities behind the negotiation. Chinese teams should see these issues as problems to be explained and mutually resolved.

TABLE 5.8 Awareness: some strong points of Chinese negotiators

Typical strong points	Comments on Chinese negotiators
Establish relationships with favors/concessions	• The Chinese side may offer small concessions or favors early in the negotiation to build the relationship. Foreign partners should respond appropriately, but care must be given not to give too much or too little in response.
Disputes resolved informally	• Allows low-cost joint problem solving while improving the relationship. Non-Chinese may not be comfortable with this process or may not have the language and culture skills to join. They should develop the skills and staff necessary to join in the process. • Chinese partners may be willing to commit resources in order to satisfy a need not covered explicitly in the contract in order to complete a project amicably.
Easy to establish good relationships	• Chinese negotiating teams generally do not have a standoffish nature. It is not too difficult to build up professional and personal connections. Doing so is likely to ease the negotiations in general and to support the kind of informal problem solving that is usual in China.
Lasting relationships	• Generally, Chinese teams will prefer to work with known companies. Thus, once a successful, satisfying relationship is in place, it may create much more value in coming years.

(Continued)

TABLE 5.8 (Continued)

Typical strong points	Comments on Chinese negotiators
In depth review	• May work through repeated lines of questions to sound out the bottom line of the other sides. With time, teams are able to gather significant insights into the business questions of the negotiation and use this to their advantage.
Tough on price	• Chinese teams have a reputation of being tough on price. However, this is not always to the joint benefit of all parties. The non-Chinese sides should point out how avoiding minimal profit margins can benefit all parties in the long term.

Choose a partner from your culture to work with. Take some time to write down some strong and weak points that you see among negotiators in your culture. Then write out comments about the strong points and advice regarding the weak points.

Some strong points of negotiators from your culture _____

Typical strong points	Comments on _____

Some weak points of negotiators from your culture _____

Typical weak points	Advice for "us"

Gender

Women may find themselves in a different position than men in a business negotiation. In some cultures, women are not taken seriously, and in some places, they may be excluded from casual business events, especially those involving alcohol. Women interviewed in the course of developing this textbook had various strategies for participating in business negotiation. Some of these are included in Table 5.9:

TABLE 5.9 Gender-related strategies

Strategy	*How it works*
Start with a serious issue	• Start communication with technical issue or a philosophical issue to establish your credibility. The owner of JBond in Tokyo, Ms. Saito, used this approach instead of the usual small talk when she was starting in the business world. This way, she could signal to upper level managers that she was a serious part of the process.
Start with a display of toughness	• Show that you are not soft and easy to deal with. Do not, however, start with an aggressive or negative style (see the section "Playing the hard card first" in Chapter 7).
Schedule casual events in advance	• Avoid late nights and distasteful entertainments by scheduling the events and locations. If you allow others to choose the restaurant or club, you may find they have picked unpleasant places.
	• Avoid extra drinking of alcohol by choosing juices or other non-alcohol cocktails as much as possible. Make a habit of immediately asking the waiter for something you like without alcohol (good advice for male and female negotiators!)
Persistence	• Some older managers may not take women, especially younger women, seriously. A good approach is to try repeatedly to get your ideas and information out. This may mean carefully stepping into the conversation or following up after a meeting with email, written documents or phone calls.
Formal stance	• Maintain a highly professional profile using language and gestures to create an atmosphere of respect. You can dress formally (but not fancily) and use formal posture and gesture. Be careful, however, not to create a barrier of formal behavior – it is also important to be appropriately accessible for information sharing and joint problem solving. Deputy US Trade Representative in Japan, Wendy Cutler, says, "Women must present themselves as firm yet pleasant" (Handover, 2014, p. 23).

(*Continued*)

TABLE 5.9 (Continued)

Strategy	How it works
Name your strategy here:	• Explain how it works here:
Name your strategy here:	• Explain how it works here:

Section summary

Gender may play itself out in a negotiation in many ways that are continuously evolving. Female and male negotiators should remain sensitive to current thinking and constantly learn about changes in current thinking on these issues.

6

TALKING THE TALK

The phrases you will use as you negotiate in business will be mainly related to the functions listed. Generally you will do more relationship building at the beginning, clarifying and summarizing throughout the talks and more information sharing before and during problem solving. Accepting, agreeing, proposing and rejecting will occur in smaller bursts at various times.

Functions include:

- relationship building;
- problem solving;
- accepting, agreeing, proposing and rejecting offers;
- summarizing and clarifying;
- breaking deadlock;
- sharing information.

The first of these, relationship building, is discussed in Chapter 2, and problem solving is discussed in Chapter 8. Setting the agenda, offers, summarizing, clarifying and sharing information are discussed in this chapter. Additionally, some practical items like setting the agenda, sharing information, handling threats and rude language are discussed in the section "Practical verbal signals".

Designing offers and suggesting tradeoffs

Regarding negotiating with Chinese people and organizations, we learn from various authorities including Irl Davis of Global One that you should ". . . try to form your negotiations with the Chinese in terms of social benefits to the Chinese" (Davis, n.d.).

TABLE 6.1 Proposals that seem to benefit the other side

Example of how not to do it . . .	Tomo: Hey, give me 1000 yen! Hiro: No!
A better way . . .	Tomo: SuperMiniPizzas are three for 1000 yen, but nine for 2000 yen, today only! If you give me 1000 yen, I will run to the shop and get a lot! Hiro: OK! I love SMPs! Here, take my money!
Or even better, Tomo can try to get a little more for himself . . .	Tomo: SuperMiniPizzas are three for 1000 yen, but nine for 2000 yen, today only! I see you are busy with your special project. If you give me 1000 yen, I will get them, but I'll keep the ninth SMP. Hiro: Sure, four instead of three is a great deal. And I can save time and get my project done before class. I am happy to give you the ninth one.

This idea may be generally true regarding China and Chinese people due to their feelings about their country and culture, sometimes called *guanxi*. However, the idea is not important to only Chinese people. Let's expand it: always show how your offer is good for the other negotiators and their interests. You do not always need to show what is good for a whole city or country, but with any counterparty, you must demonstrate that your proposal is good for the individuals, good for the organization they represent and good for their interests.

Make your offers appealing – give the other side an incentive to accept your offer.

Now it's your turn – work in pairs

First, student A

Student A: You have already agreed that Student B will buy 10,000 units from you for $10,000, including delivery and labels. Now try to get a higher price for changing the label to include B's photograph – it will cost you $500, so try to get more than a five percent increase in total price.

Make an offer using a sentence that shows it is good for student B.

Now, student B

Student B: You just learned you can deliver the 10,000 units efficiently for only $1,000, and you know that delivery will cost A $1,500. Try to get a discount from student A of at least $1,000 on the existing $10,000 agreement.

Make an offer using a sentence that shows it is good for student A.

Offer design: ask for specific things, offer less specific things in exchange

Keep your flexibility when you make an offer. Ask the other side to do something clearly so you can be sure of what you are getting. But make your concession less clear so you can change a little.

Even better – show what is good for OtsuTech and ask them for a specific point leaving some flexibility for yourself.

TABLE 6.2 Compare the proposals

Version A	Version B
Tomo: SuperMiniPizzas are three for 1000 yen, but nine for 2000 yen, today only! If you give me 1000 yen, I will run to the shop and get a lot! Hiro: OK! I love SMPs! Here, take my money!	Tomo: SuperMiniPizzas are three for 1000 yen, but nine for 2000 yen, today only! If you give me 1000 yen, I will run to the shop and bring half for you! Hiro: OK! I love SMPs! Here, take my money!
Which offer is better designed for Tomo? Why?	

TABLE 6.3 Best design of proposal

Version A	Version B
XinFab: We can decrease the price by 5 percent if you would consider improving our delivery schedule. OtsuTech: That sounds OK. We can let you deliver at the start of March instead of the end of February.	XinFab: We could decrease the price by a few percentage points if you let us deliver after 10 March instead of at the end of February. OtsuTech: That sounds OK.
Which offer is better designed for XinFab? Why? Write your ideas here.	

> XinFab: We can save you some money! We will decrease the price a few percentage points if you let us deliver after 12 March instead of at the end of February.
>
> OtsuTech: That sounds OK.
> XinFab: How about 2.5 percent?

Core language of offers

If you give us *(specific thing)* , we will consider giving you *(not very specific thing)* .
    Note: This is a review of the same points regarding language that you can find in the section on counteroffers.

Write a sentence or two making offers that are a little better for you, but acceptable for the other side

1.   Offer your hotel event services at a price 5 percent higher than normal to the conference planning committee of IBM Japan.

    _____
    _____
    _____

2.   Offer a power conversion technology for 5 percent more than the usual price for such technology.

    _____
    _____
    _____

Offers and counteroffers

- "How about . . ."
- "We can do it for $6,000 per month."
- "We can't do it for less than $6,000 per month."
- "We'd like to suggest . . ."
- "Would you be interested in . . ."
- "We propose . . ."

A good counteroffer includes an idea about changes or exchanges, but not a detailed exchange. Let the details develop as you learn more about what you can give and receive.

Good

If you agree to grant us exclusive rights for the United Kingdom, then we will rethink our promotional calendar for the forthcoming year.

Bad

We will give your product lead feature every month in our promotional calendar for the next year if you give us exclusive rights for the United Kingdom.

Adapted from *Bare Knuckle Negotiating* (Hazeldine, 2006, pp. 77–78).

Try to do it like this

> If you give us __(specific thing)__, we will consider giving you ___(less specific thing)__
>
> If your side is willing to provide the product 2 percent cheaper on the last day of the month, we might be able to increase our total order. Is that possible for your side?
>
> Examples:
>
> - "If you _____, I will rethink . . ."
> - "If you _____, we will reconsider . . ."
> - "If you _____, I can look at . . ."
> - "If you _____, I can rethink . . ."
> - "If you _____, we can explore . . ."

In the previous example, notice that the "good" version allows the offerer to give more (and receive more). The "bad" version allows no chance for expansion because something specific is being confirmed with no future opportunity for developing, sharing or retaining that specific point.

Package and repackage your offers

As you make offers, bring together parts of the whole deal in different ways. This effort at packaging and repackaging will help you and your counterparties to find the best fitting deal. This process is very important in complicated integrative deals. Talking through the choices and scenarios is likely to increase trust, satisfaction and value.

Section summary

> 1) Help the other parties understand why your proposal is good.
> 2) Ask for something specific but carefully offer something less specific, then continue negotiating.

Accepting and rejecting

Firm acceptance

- "Sounds good!"
- "We agree."
- "That looks like a fine idea."
- "Let's do it."
- "We have no problem with that."
- "That's a green light."
- "That works for us."
- "I can do that."
- "I'll go for that."
- "Good idea."
- "I can manage that."

Tentative acceptance

- "That may be alright . . . we will have to check with headquarters."
- "That sounds like it is in the right range, but let's talk about it more."
- "That's a starting point . . ."
- "We may be able to agree with . . ."
- "Now we are in the ballpark." (The price is close to the target.)

Firm rejection

When you hear these, you should carefully get more information but be prepared for no agreement on the issue. Notice that some of these seem tentative, but are firm.

- "That's not possible for us."
- "No way."
- "No can do."
- "That would be a deal breaker."
- "That's a show stopper from our point of view."
- "The cost is much too high."
- "I don't think so."
- "That's not quite what I was thinking."

Referring to causes outside the company usually shows that there can be no change or discussion about a topic.

Examples:

- "The end users have made it clear they will not buy a product this color."
- "The government has recently changed the regulations and all our products will have to be 10cm wider."

A firm rejection may show the "reserve" position of that topic. Probe a little more to be sure.

Poorly designed rejection

Notice that this following rejection is much weaker because the rules are inside the company:

> "...we've got a problem with these because our [internal] rules have changed again since ..."

(Vuorela, 2005, p. 54)

This is a weak rejection because it is almost certainly possible to suggest that the negotiators return to their company for permission to change the situation. They could even make a phone call right away. If they refuse, it might be that they were faking and do not have any rules about this. Or they might make the rejection more firm (and more clearly real). A weak rejection might mean that they are playing for time because they need to discuss or rethink their position. If this seems to be the case, propose taking a break.

Tentative rejection

When you hear these, you should explore more ideas, get more information and hope for an agreement.

- "We would like to consider that and discuss it more at our next meeting."
- "The cost is a little higher than we were expecting ..."
- "We'll have to ask headquarters about it."
- "Our budget really can't handle that."
- "I don't think my boss will like it."
- "We will have to look into it ..."
- "I think there might be room to maneuver on that ..."
- "I will have to check with my boss ..."
- "My idea is a little different."

These tentative rejections usually suggest that you will be able to agree with more discussion, understanding and maybe concessions.

Summarizing and clarifying

Summarizing/confirming

In *Bare Knuckle Negotiating*, Hazeldine (2006) says "summarize frequently" so that all parties are clear about the details and what they agree and disagree about. Frequent summarizing helps all parties maintain a good relationship and clear ideas about the process.

Here are some examples:

> *So that's* $5,000 for each delivery, payable five business days in advance by electronic transfer, right?
>
> *If I got it right*, you mean shipping to on the last day of the month and paying by the fifth business day of the month, right?
>
> *To review*, our idea so far is to decrease by 9 percent during the first three months in three equal steps . . . is that right?
>
> *I gather that* your position is a little different from ours, so if we increased by 5% you would not be satisfied.

Summarizing, confirming and reviewing means that a negotiation usually goes in circles and loops. It does not usually move forward on a straight line. Figure 6.1 gives a reasonable view of the messy real world of negotiation.

Clarification

> Do I understand that . . . ?
> What do you mean?
> Could you explain that in more detail?

Linear approach – one issue resolved after another in good order.

Looks nice, but the real world is not so simple.

Looping approach – issues resolved, then reviewed, perhaps changed.

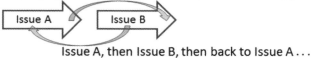

Issue A, then Issue B, then back to Issue A . . .

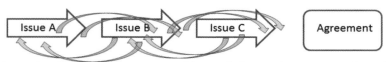

In reality, looping is messy, repetitive and slow . . . but gets good results because ideas are confirmed, developed, reviewed, changed and reconfirmed.

FIGURE 6.1 The messy reality of the negotiation progress

How would that work with the other product?

So this plan is indeed technically feasible; is that correct?

I don't know if I understood that correctly, could you rephrase the idea?

Practical verbal signals

How do you know if the other side is interested in knowing more or has no more interest in agreeing? Understanding the meaning of certain words and phrases may help. This section includes examples of words and phrases that signal feelings. Earlier in this chapter, we saw how to make offers using words and phrases that are positive-sounding and flexible. In this section, we see that careful verbal signals can show that either you or the other side is willing to negotiate a point.

It is important to structure your signal so that the hint of movement on your part is conditional on the other party responding positively. . . . You imply a willingness to negotiate, but only if the other party reciprocates.

"Our normal price is X." this could be a signal that although the normal price is X, under certain circumstances, the possibility of a different price exists.

Bare Knuckle Negotiating, Hazeldine, p. 66

"It would be incredibly difficult for us to accept an agreement of less than five years in duration." This signals the possibility of movement. You are indicating that there is the possibility of flexibility. You are not saying that you will agree to an agreement of less than five years – you are signaling that you are prepared to discuss it. The use of the word "difficult" implies that the other party will need to provide some incentive for you to make some movement. . . . You are inviting the other party to move the negotiation forward.

. . . encourage them to expand . . . "Under what circumstances would you be able to alter the specification?"

"How could I make it easier for you to agree to the proposed fee?"

Bare Knuckle Negotiating, Hazeldine, p. 72

To summarize, the best signals invite a concession from the other side before you have made a clear offer.

Playing for time

These phrases are useful when you need a little time to think.

"I see."

"Could you explain that to me in a little more detail?"

"Could you repeat the first part of that idea?"

"It sounds like an interesting idea, could you run through the main points for
me again?"

"Let's take a break."

"I'd like to sleep on that."

The most useful phrase for getting time, of course, is, "We'd like to discuss that
internally – how about if we take a break?"

Too expensive

"This is above our budget."

"Our expectations about cost were very different."

"We are feeling some sticker shock."

Better than we expected

Immediate agreement to a price usually indicates that the other side was worried
about a worse price. It may be difficult to improve the price (from your point of
view) after an answer like this.

We are interested in this issue

Echo questions (see Chapter 2) usually indicate strong interest or a desire to learn
more about that topic.

Setting the agenda

Negotiators must agree about the first general topic and its subtopics when they
begin to talk. They must agree to an agenda. This can be done face-to-face or in the
days ahead by phone, email or other method. Follow Table 6.4 to see how agenda
setting works after the greeting.

This conversation could go a different way – Red could push a little more and
get their topics on the agenda first.

TABLE 6.4 Agenda setting

Action	Say	Comment
Set the general topic	I'd like to talk about *GB Joint Venture*. We think the joint venture is a good starting point to make some positive agreements, is that alright?	Agree to what you will start with. Be flexible – if they want to start with a different issue, it is OK unless the sequence is very illogical.
Specify topics	In that case, let's discuss the ownership structure, the decision making balance and . . .	Briefly agree regarding what you will include in this conversation (subtopics).

Action	Say	Comment
State position(s)	We think the price of _____ should be about _____ because . . . (it is good for you)	Also quickly start the price conversation (high side if selling, low side if buying). Always give a reason with a price – a reason that sounds and feels good for them.
Link or delink	That sounds good, but we would like to talk about the third one, _____, later because _____. Is that OK?	If you do not want to include a particular point, suggest handling it later.
Discuss positions	We agree about ____, but we think ____.	Talk openly and freely. Listen closely to understand what they want. Work on details.
Summarize	So if I understand right, we all think the price should be _____ and include _____, _____ and _____.	Summarize frequently and finally agree.
Move to next topic	Let's move on to _____	
Repeat all of above		

TABLE 6.5 Sample dialog for setting the agenda

Blue: Hello – we are glad to meet again regarding our successful JV! We have some fresh ideas about making our cooperation even better.	Greeting (Blue even sets the topic here)
Red: Yes, glad to see you all again.	Greeting
Blue: We would like to talk first about the JV – that is a set of issues we can easily manage together. Let's include restructuring ownership, decision making and expanding the JV. Is that alright?	Topic, subtopics (Blue sets the topic/agenda)
Red: Yes, but what about the decision making, we don't see how that is a question . . .	Subtopics
Blue: We will explain – it's a small issue that fits well with everything. First we understand that Red will benefit from a 60/40 ownership ratio. That will save you a lot of taxes, and a little for us too. Basically, we agree! But because we don't want a simple "technology transfer" operation (we want a real JV), we would like to share decision making power 50/50.	Subtopics (confirmed with reason)
Red: That is a little unusual. Can you explain what you are thinking?	Question for information
Blue: Sure, we . . . (explains)	Explanation, discussion
Red: I see. We can agree to that, though it is a little difficult and will generate some legal costs, so we propose $350,000.	Counter offer with reason
Blue: We can agree to a reasonable discount for the trouble. But we admit our initial price was high – for a reason. The reason is that . . .	Back to high price and explanation

Moving to a new topic

Let's turn to Issue 3, please. The topic here is whether or not to continue . . .
(Page 120 of arbitration transcript, Ohio State)

I see. And I'm not really an expert on this subject, *so we'll move on.*
(Page 144 of arbitration transcript, Ohio State)

Responding to threats

In a negotiation, you may hear a range of threats to your position. Some are acceptable and some are unacceptable.

Note: the best way to react to a threat is to respond directly with facts. A direct response will show clearly that you can react and continue the conversation instead of giving in to the demand. Alternatively, you can respond with silence while waiting for the threat-making side to make the next move. When you respond with silence, your silence is a signal that you are not satisfied with the offer or threat.

Your counterparts probably do not really want to end the negotiation, so you do not have to give in to threats in order to save the deal. If the other side really wants to end the negotiation, let them end it; remember, their BATNA must be good enough that they can walk away. If your BATNA is strong enough, you can walk away and find a new negotiation partner that does not make threats.

For more on tactics and responding to negative tactics, see Chapter 7.

Making threats

Don't make unacceptable threats at all. Even acceptable threats should be kept to a minimum by companies engaged in productive talks that will lead to greater future cooperation. Acceptable threats are not good tools for building relationships.

TABLE 6.6 Acceptable and unacceptable threats

Acceptable	Unacceptable
"We will have to compare your offer to your competitors."	"If you don't agree to this, we will go directly to your competitor and you will never survive in this business."
"Your timing does not suit us. We might give that part of the contract to XY Corp."	"We'll damage your relationship with your main customer if you don't agree to this."
Comment	
Acceptable threats do not suggest any significant danger to the business or personal trouble to the other party. These are acceptable and within the range of normal business.	Unacceptable threats reach beyond the immediate business talks and suggest serious damage, even personal damage, to the other party.

Rude, vulgar, taboo

These words may be used casually and can even help to relax a formal or tense atmosphere. However, generally you should avoid words that are considered rude, vulgar and taboo. This is especially good advice for non-native speakers of English who may not be able to use the words correctly. If your counterparties use these words, try to determine if they are intentionally being casual or if they are genuinely upset. If they are truly upset, look for ways to decrease the tension.

Deadlock and breaking deadlock

Sometimes parties in a negotiation cannot agree. This situation is called deadlock. If deadlock happens to you, you have a few possible actions:

1. Leave the topic temporarily and come back to it later;
2. Cut the issue out of the negotiation permanently;
3. Link the topic creatively to another topic, action or concession;
4. Make a new try with other contacts (different people at the counterparty's organization, different staff on the negotiation teams, removing yourself from the team, etc.);
5. Develop a backchannel contact – a person in the organization who is not directly related to the topic matter (note: this may be seen as underhanded or tricky, especially in business);
6. Agree to an independent fact finder who can decide on a specific problem, such as a price evaluation;
7. Agree to a set of rules that can be used impartially by all sides;
8. Consider alternative dispute resolution (ADR) methods such as mediation or arbitration. See Chapter 10 for more on the subject of ADR.

Of course, if the deadlock cannot be broken and the issue cannot be abandoned, you or the other side may have to use your BATNA.

What to say when deadlock occurs

- I think we are becoming stuck on this topic, let's move on to . . .
- Seems like we are stuck, how about a break before we continue with another issue?
- It seems like we can't agree about this, so let's talk about another topic and come back to this later. Is that OK?
- After two hours we still disagree, how about removing this from the negotiations and asking an independent party to decide?
- We clearly disagree about who made the mistake, so let's find a judge who can decide clearly about it. In the meantime, let's continue talking about . . .
- We frankly cannot pay more than $12,500 for the equipment. However, we could pay a little more for the installation if you allow us to select the work team . . . what do you think?
- Is it possible to do that work under some limited or special conditions?

Another approach – consider the points in the problem issue that you can understand

Fisher and Shapiro (2005) suggest that a negotiator take a neutral position temporarily while communicating with the other parties about a troublesome issue. If there are points in the issue that you can understand, it may help the other side to appreciate your points after you have demonstrated that you understand their points.

Deadlock 1

Think about the following deadlock situation and suggest how the negotiators could manage. Write out the sentences they could use.

Company A wants to sell Company B's motorcycle tires, but not their accessories. Company B strongly wants A to sell both tires and accessories. After 20 minutes, they are deadlocked.

_____

_____

Deadlock 2

Recall the case of the incompetent translator in Chapter 1. What could the project manager have done to bring the translator into a negotiation? Would it be worth the time and cost?

_____

_____

_____

Section summary

> Creative ideas and links to other issues are best for breaking deadlocks, but it is not always possible. Identifying unresolvable deal-breaking deadlock issues in advance will save time and cost.

Shutdown moves

How can you bring a negotiation to an end at the right time?

In his book *Negotiauctions*, Subramanian (2010) of Harvard Business School describes shutdown moves as a way to prevent the other side(s) from finding better deals with competitors. Subramanian also points out that timing is important – shutdown moves must appear when the other side is close to accepting and delay would result in their reconsideration of alternatives.

You may have to make these more moves than once – Subramanian tells us that only 20 percent of attempts are immediately successful.

TABLE 6.7 Shutdown moves

Move	Language example	Comment
Conditional agreements	If we agree today, we can speed delivery time by 10 percent for no cost.	These shutdown moves can create value and convenience for all parties. It is possible to make these too restrictive and therefore unappealing. Design these moves carefully.
Appealing release terms	If we agree now, we will release you from the agreement if oil prices rise 5 percent more than expected this year.	
Acceptable penalty clauses	You can break the agreement by paying a 5 percent fee any time in the first four weeks.	
Direct appeal	It looks like we have covered all the issues well, can you agree with the deal as it is?	If the parties are basically satisfied, this move can bring a close to the deal with no more time lost.
Compare benefits	Let's review the proposal in detail. (List the benefits to all parties in detail, possibly in spreadsheet format.)	This move appeals to negotiators who appreciate rights and fairness. If a party has a Win/Lose mindset, emphasize the "better" value they are getting.
Extra strong moral position	If you agree now, we can deliver these medicines immediately and help those people!	This kind of shutdown move is unreasonable. Do not rush into an agreement. Avoid using this kind of shutdown move.
Split the difference	We have come so far, how about we meet in the middle?	This move catches tired negotiators who may have lost track of where the "middle" really is. Instead, share resources or repackage until both sides have satisfying benefits.
A spoonful of sugar	If we sign off now, I will make sure that your logo is at the entrance all week – for free.	A late small concession that is highly visible can sometimes bring the negotiations to a close. However, if the deal does not close, the concession may be forfeited and lose its special appeal.
Time restrictions	Our offer is only open until the stock market starts on Monday morning – we must have an agreement by then.	These are ultimatums. Do not accept, just coolly reevaluate. See the section on tactics.
Ultimatums	Agree now or we will withdraw the offer!	Avoid using these.

Section summary

Time your shutdown moves carefully to complete phases of a negotiation or the whole thing. Polite persistence may be necessary.

Language choice

Choice of language in negotiation

This textbook is in English and provides practical advice about choice of words and phrases in English. But much of the advice will be useful in situations that use only a little English or no English at all. In business negotiations with more than one culture, the participants may pick a common language that some or all know well and they may mix one or more other languages with the common one.

Negotiators can choose the language to match the agenda. Interviews quoting cross-functional team members from a multinational enterprise in the IT industry (Chen, 2008) show the process.

Huang, a Chinese native language speaker in Vancouver, Canada, uses English as a foreign . . . and as a corporate language within her firm. She describes the dilemma of using languages while managing tasks and social-relations.

International companies rely on multilingual speakers to find the best solution for both parties . . . language is not a big problem when we only talk about logistic issues . . . but when a work problem becomes personal, using a foreign language to deal with relational problem becomes a major issue.

(Huang, personal communication, 2013)

Two points are of interest. First, multilingual negotiators choose between a native and a foreign language to negotiate with the same native language speakers. Second, the choice of language impacts the message receiver's own perception. The choice of language can be a tool for maintaining or removing old divisions or for creating new ones during collective actions.

Use of multiple languages in negotiation

Negotiating with those who share the same native languages

Multilingual negotiators from the same native language background should concern the effects of language choices when prioritizing task-based negotiation or relational-orientation negotiation. When negotiators are grounded in a common environment (e.g., nation, culture, institution), their language options can include local and corporate languages (or native and foreign languages).

The examples that follow show how this happens in day-to-day work.

- Kao, a Chinese native language speaker, uses her corporate language, English, as a foreign common language in a firm based in Taipei, Taiwan where the local languages include Mandarin and Taiwanese. She describes how negotiators use language socially while coordinating tasks. Her statement shows how negotiators use their native language and how they react to a foreign LF.

  I use Chinglish, it is a mixture of Chinese and English. . . . I like to add 'ah, la, oh' these kind of sound in English . . . to be more expressive. When my Taiwanese counterparts speak in English only, it occasionally makes me feel they have some kind of attitude, snobbish or demanding . . . maybe distant.
  (Kao, personal communication, 2013)

- Ma, a Chinese native language speaker in Vancouver, Canada, uses a foreign language – English. He describes how common native language speakers use a foreign language to conceal cognitive implication and present appropriate social actions in negotiation. He describes how language choice is a trade-off.

  It's hard to use a foreign language to show feelings with my fellows . . . no emotion exchange, it's easier to make progress when I make a point about company policy, but things may become personal and damage relationships . . . for a long-term work project, bad relationship makes our team loose . . . whole project would be jeopardized.
  (Ma, personal communication, 2013)

Switching between different languages to create a multilingual context can be a negotiation strategy. Negotiators choose languages to develop aspects of the negotiation such as relationships and joint understanding.

Negotiations when there is no shared native language

Negotiators from various countries may or may not share a common native language. Yet, in a single-language environment, a foreign common language requires greater demands than using a native language. The sole use of a foreign language causes difficulties in sharing information and impacts relationship processes by adding complexity (Salk and Brannen, 2000).

> Liang, a Chinese native language speaker in Vancouver, Canada, uses a foreign language, English. He describes how he uses it to negotiate with Canadians and how the choice of a foreign language can influence value-claiming.
>
> *My Canadian counterparts know that I am Chinese and English is not my mother tongue. The good thing of negotiating in English is that English native language speakers will be more tolerant of my directness. Sometimes I can be rude and strongly express my opinion. They could simply interpret my style or attitude is more like a cultural barrier. So, they are more likely to focus on how to get the work done.*
>
> (Liang, personal communication, 2013)

Multiple language choices give negotiators strategic alternatives. Negotiators may select, switch and mix languages to transfer information, build relationships or show their intentions.

> Lin (in Xiamen, China) explains how multilingual negotiators utilize a foreign common language even when they communicate with their counterparts who speak the same native language to prioritize task-oriented issues.
>
> *In negotiation, we manage different conflicts, such as issues relating task or issues jeopardizing relationship. English is like a tool to focus on work, such as a firm's policies, task requirements, subject titles, as well as a way to detach my personal feelings to be assertive.*
>
> (Lin, personal communication, 2013)

The quote suggests that multilingual actors are sensitive to the choice of language in a negotiation. When negotiators choose a foreign language over their common native language to express their feelings, they may experience difficulty.

In the following example, a native English and a native Chinese speaker switch between the languages. They use Chinese and English to build up the relationship, but mainly English for the technical issues, except for one offer.

> Both Go-si and Grant work in different firms. Go-si is Chinese, based in Beijing, China and Grant is Canadian, based in Shenzhen, China. They both switch between native and foreign languages – Chinese and English.
>
> Go-si: Grant! I need to discuss something with you. Are you available now?
> Grant: She me shi? (Translation: What to discuss?)

> Go-si: You know that we need to quickly despatch our products to your sides, however, due to the budget issues, we would like to change to courier delivery instead of using flight cargo. Is it okay? I will despatch the products two days earlier, but it will be four days late if that is okay with your side?
>
> Grant: Hmm . . . let me check. . . . I am not sure about it. We have other deadline to catch here. What's the problem?
>
> Go-si: We had some problems on one of our operational lines. So, we need to redo some work. However, if we can change the delivery method, we may be able to reduce extra financial costs. Anything you can suggest?
>
> Grant: Yi ban huo chen yi ban kung yun? What do you think? (Translation: Half delivery by courier, and half by flight cargo?)
>
> Go-si: Great! Xie le :D (Translation: Thanks for that!)
>
> Grant: Bu ke qi ☺ (Translation: You are welcome.)
>
> (Go-si and Grant, personal communication, 2013)

The Canadian (Grant) uses his counterpart's native language (Chinese) to benefit his counterpart. This approach indicates a clear intention to deepen social relations with the other businessperson. Even though the Chinese native language speaker (Go-si) prefers the foreign language to actually process the task, he responds to Grant by switching to Chinese. In this way, Go-si recognizes his counterpart's attempt to deepen their social bond. A negotiator can uses his/her counterpart's native language in order to socially connect and develop a closer bond.

Section summary

> When negotiation participants are from different language backgrounds, or even the same language background but operating in a foreign environment, choice of different languages will have important impact.

Visual communication

It is not necessary to communicate by speaking and writing only. A business negotiation can be an opportunity for very broad communication, especially during problem-solving discussions. Using visual communication can support the ability of the parties to communicate and create solutions.

Q. What is visual communication?

A. Using pictures, diagrams, sketches, models, skits, charts, etc. to share ideas and solve problems. These things can be casual or professional, prepared in advance or created on the spot. They can be made by one person or all parties.

Q. Why should we bother with visual communication? After all, speaking works well, and drawing bad pictures does not seem very professional.
A. Visual communication improves on spoken communication in three aspects of negotiation according to Swaab, Postmes, Neijens, Kiers and Dumay (2002):

- understanding;
- relationship;
- satisfaction.

Further, joint creation of images can lead to joint problem solving, which also supports understanding, relationship and satisfaction.

Q. Which do you think is better for a face-to-face negotiation: a whiteboard or a computer and projector?
A. Your answer: _____

_____

Presentations

Presentations are for delivering information in one direction. Negotiations, however, combine input from all parties. Therefore, a presentation is usually not appropriate for a negotiation. If you feel an introductory presentation is useful, keep it short and simple. The slides should be uncluttered, but not black and white. Use animations, images, diagrams, maps, video, graphs and tables more than words. Note: animations must be simple, not complicated, not distracting and not overly cute. In any case, bring the presentation on paper in case of technical problems.

Handouts

Handouts are much more suitable for a business negotiation than presentations. Handouts can be reviewed in any order, at any time, by all parties. All parties can contribute their ideas to the handout simply by writing on it. Each handout can focus on a single point. More information can be delivered and developed by use of handouts than through presentations.

How to make useful drawings and diagrams on paper or whiteboard

Dan Roam (2010) in *The Back of the Napkin* suggests that you consider five dimensions when you want to visually communicate. These dimensions are:

- Simple v. Elaborate
- Quality v. Quantity

- Vision v. Execution
- Individual v. Compare
- Change v. As-is

The Back of the Napkin, Roam, 2010

Understanding these five issues will help you quickly decide what kind of image to draw, what the focus of your communication should be and how to draw it.

- Use a simple picture to communicate only about that object, but draw an elaborate picture to show the object in its context (use, origin, users, transportation, etc.)
- Draw a quality picture to discuss a detailed characteristic of an object. Quantity pictures include graphs, charts, and numbers.
- If your idea is about the final outcome of a new business activity, draw a vision picture that shows things as they will be. A vision picture might show customers using the product and how it solves their problems. If your idea is about the processes necessary to create a new business activity, draw an execution picture showing the steps. An execution picture might be a process diagram or flow chart with lines and arrows.
- Individual pictures show one object, but in order to compare, you should draw more than one object. With several drawings, you can point out individual differences, for example, the meaning of quality in apples (size, shape, bites, bruises, etc.)
- Your drawing might show a change or the as-is situation. As-is pictures show the object or idea as it works (or does not work) now. The change picture shows how the system would be in the future.

Summary: choose the picture or short series of pictures that will be the most useful for you. Make simple drawings because they are quick and effective. You will improve your communication ability with practice, but the goal is not to draw nice pictures, just to communicate!

As an answer to the earlier question about whether a whiteboard or computer is better suited for a situation, consider Table 6.8.

TABLE 6.8 Comparing visual media

Whiteboard	Computer
Many can access it simultaneously	Only one person at a time
Easily used and modified	May not be easy to draw complex ideas
Skills widely available	Slow typing or weak graphics skills will harm the process
Promotes co-creation	Blocks joint use
Builds relationship	Tends toward struggles for control of machine
Not hard to save (photograph and process later)	Easy to save and distribute

With only one plus point on the computer side, the advantages are heavily in favor of doing the work by hand. Advice to co-create with counterparties:

- share the paper and pens;
- use a whiteboard;
- stick figures and non-beautiful drawings are OK;
- bring a few colored pencils/markers (too many colors will lead to confusion);
- keep it simple and short (KISS).

Practice a little to improve your skills, but don't worry too much!

Conclusion

Use whiteboards, prepared graphics and diagrams, photos, video, animations, sticky notes, notepaper on the table or even paper napkins. Visual communication supports problem solving, idea sharing and relationship building.

Remote and electronic negotiations

Not all negotiations are face-to-face. Email and teleconferencing may make it impossible to share the use of a whiteboard or paper. In that case, it is possible to encourage joint problem solving by sharing documents through collaboration software. See the next section in this chapter for more information on remote negotiations.

Section summary

> Use visualizations of all sorts to facilitate communication of ideas in negotiation – these support the verbal negotiation and are generally accepted as serious.

Remote electronic negotiations

Increasingly the business world negotiates partly or entirely by remote media: video, phone and email. These tools are convenient and accessible – a smart phone might be enough for all of these. The advantages of remote electronic talks include convenience and speed. The disadvantages include having less context around the talk: facial expressions, voice tone, gestures and so on. These clues are minimized or cut out completely in remote negotiations, and it becomes easier to miscommunicate. We can describe media on a scale between rich (lots of context and information) to poor (little information other than the core message), as in Figure 6.2.

Use rich media for complex discussions, emotional content and new relationships. Use poor media for simpler content with established relationships. Figure 6.3 suggests which form of communication to choose depending on the relationship and the complexity of the issues.

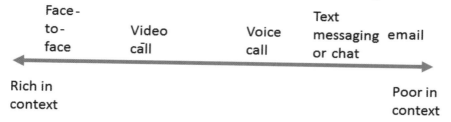

FIGURE 6.2 Rich and poor context media

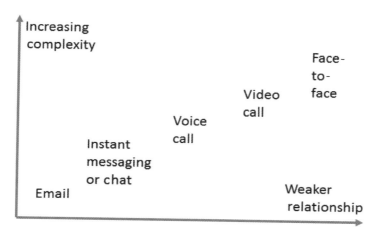

FIGURE 6.3 Which medium fits best

Email advantages

According to Figure 6.2 and 6.3, email and text messaging are the media that carry the least context information. Email, unlike text messaging, does not even tell the users if a person is available or not. With so little context, there are some advantages to be exploited:

- No instant response needed (asynchronous)
  Email does not require an immediate response – it can wait for minutes or days at your convenience. After opening an email, you can take time to gather information and consider alternatives before answering.
- Language skills
  If the negotiating parties do not share the same native language, email allows for slow responses with time to create and revise in the foreign language. This slow process is much more comfortable (and more grammatically accurate) than the immediate give and take of live communication. Language learners benefit from email's low–pressure format.

- Low barrier

  Some people feel more comfortable proposing an idea when it is not face-to-face or using live media. Email provides the feeling of insulation from a poorly promoted proposal (author research, Chen, 2008).

  Additionally, low power individuals may communicate more and more successfully using email or messaging (Thompson, 2012).

- Manage emotions

  Email does not necessarily show emotions, especially if you take time creating and revising it. You can manage your display of emotions to make the recipient think you are happy, angry, satisfied, etc. On the other hand, it is easy for email to be misread by recipients who project their own emotions or worries onto the email. Therefore, extra care in writing, careful use of emoticons and follow up calls and visits may be wise.

Define a clear purpose for your email

If your email's purpose remains uncertain, the message may be misunderstood or even remain unread. Therefore, the person responsible for writing the email needs to explicitly and clearly address the key points during the introduction to motivate the recipient(s) to carry on reading and get the point. However, if the introduction is overly long or unclear, the reader may lose focus or skip passages of text and miss or overlook one or more key points. Therefore, an informative subject line and brief introduction are the best combination.

Don't waste your time writing something that won't get read. Make it easy for your recipient(s) to know what you require and expect from them. A clear and concise introduction, respectfully phrased, can help an email recipient understand the key points.

Types of email

Five kinds of email can be generalized. The type should be stated as early in the email as possible to help the reader(s) quickly identify the nature of the text and whether it is of interest. The five types of email are:

- Information sharing: conveys information without the need for a response, such as sales advertisements, reminders, etc. Avoid lengthy, excessive texts. Be explicit – help the reader understand who, what, where, when, etc. Identify the topic clearly and share the information concisely.
- Inquiries: requests advice or provides answers to questions. Responding to inquiries helps the sender gather information that may be advantageous to all parties. Number the questions and encourage a thorough response. Do not ask many questions in one email. Limit or avoid open-ended and vague questions.

- Required actions: communicates that taking action toward an issue is required to move an agenda forward. Actions include forwarding an email, linking to a webpage, receiving/checking attached files, etc.
- Open-ended discussion: opens a dialogue to keep communication active for the purpose of a mutual benefit or a future interaction. Discussions include brainstorming, project development, etc.
- Advice: If a sender requests advice on a problem, replying with a vague or an irrelevant comment (e.g. complaints) is likely to delay matters. It is important to offer concise suggestions. Generally it is a good practice to include links to supporting sources. Because advising and problem solving is a complex process, it is good to propose a phone call or face-to-face conversation.

Structure of successful email

1. Subject line – never send an email without an informative subject line. Six or fewer words is best. The topic and your general feeling or opinion should be clear.
2. Greeting – always start with the name(s) of the intended recipient(s). For example: "Dear Bob," or "Bob," or for a group, "Bob, Tom, and Susan,". You can also start "Dear Team," "Dear All," etc.
3. Lead to the next communication – In successful business, one activity leads to another. Finish up with phrases like ". . . please send me your response. . . ." ". . . let me know your opinion about . . ." ". . . I will call tomorrow to talk about the details . . ." ". . . please review the attached document and send it . . ." or ". . . I'll be in your district on Thursday, let's discuss this further over a coffee. . . ." Assertively and politely stating the date and/or time when a response needed is most likely to result in a timely reply.
4. Closing – close with a polite ending. "Best regards, Tom" is a good general-purpose ending or "Thank you, Tom". Avoid "Sincerely, Tom" or overly warm closings. "Thanks" is acceptable for an internal email in an established business relationship. After your name, a business email should include a few lines (about four) with your organization and contact information.

TABLE 6.9 Business email dos and don'ts

Content	Do	Don't
Abbreviations	Use only business abbreviations known to your readers. Explain new abbreviations as necessary.	Do not use casual ones like "CUL8er" (see you later)
Animation	Never. Especially, do not use animated emoticons.	

(Continued)

TABLE 6.9 (Continued)

Content	Do	Don't
Attachments	Yes, if format is important. Yes, if the communication is long. Yes, if you need to send graphics/images, etc.	Do not send attachments that are not directly related to the topic. Do not include company logos as attachments – put them in the body of the email if required only.
Clipart	Avoid.	
Complex issues	Make a phone call or a face-to-face visit.	Do not use email for complex issues.
Emoticons	Use sparingly. Use emoticons only to show an upbeat feeling, a concern or other very clear, simple feeling. These are generally OK in an established business relationship: ☺ :-) :) ☹ :-(:(	No animated emoticons. No unusual emoticons. No emoticons for complicated nuanced feelings Be careful, as the following are common in East Asia but are not yet common elsewhere in business: > < (^o^)
Grammar	Keep it simple.	Do not show off your grammar skills.
Humor	Avoid.	
Irony	Do not use.	
Length	Good email is short, 5–20 lines if possible. Keep it short and simple.	Do not fail to provide enough context.
Persuasion	Try to include only two support points. Generally, one point gets through and two points might get through, but more rarely get through.	Don't make it long and bothersome.
Rude/taboo words	Never.	
Sarcasm	Do not use.	

- Completeness – help the reader understand who, what, where, when, etc. In face-to-face communication or in other situations, it is easy to gather related information to the core message. However, email lacks this additional context and may be read much later when the surrounding details are no longer fresh. Therefore, identify yourself and the topic clearly. When responding to an email, keep any previous email(s) in your response.
- Clarity – avoid complicated grammar. Keep it simple.
- Simplicity – avoid complicated and delicately nuanced ideas. Keep it simple. If you have much to communicate, do it face-to-face, by phone or in a longer attached document with supporting information.
- Only one main subject – discuss only one main topic in one email. Send a new email for any new topic.

- Try to include only two or three support points, if possible. Why? The reader may not have the time or focus to manage more. The authors' experience is that "one point gets through, two might get through, more rarely get through." This is especially true for high-level managers who often simply do not have time for more than minimal and clear communications.
- Length – keep it short.

Casual abbreviations

As a rule, do not use casual abbreviations, even in casual email. These change frequently and therefore may easily be misunderstood. Some are funny, but some are quite rude. Never use a rude one in your emails or other writing. From the following list, ASAP, COB and FYI are widely used in business. You must recognize some of these, but avoid them in general.

ASAP – as soon as possible
COB – close of business (usually means 5 pm)
FYI – for your information
LOL – laugh out loud
OMG – oh my god
ROFL – roll on floor laughing
W84it – wait for it
IMHO – in my honest opinion
IIRC – if I recall correctly
FUBAR – damaged beyond all repair

Some last points of email etiquette

- Use common business acronyms and jargon with other professionals who know them – it will show that you are also professional.
- Do not use slang and local abbreviations in business email at all.
- If you are forwarding or reposting a message you've received, do not change the wording. You may shorten the message and quote only relevant parts, but be sure to properly identify the source.
- In order to ensure that people know who you are, be sure to include a line or two at the end of your message with contact information. Keep it short – no more than four lines.
- A single address may go to a group, even though the address looks like it is just one person. Know to whom you are sending!
- Be careful about cc's when replying. Do not accidentally exclude people. Also, do not continue to include extra people if the messages have become a two-way conversation.
- Do not write with all capital letters. IT LOOKS AS IF YOU'RE SHOUTING ANGRILY. This is true for email and all writing. Do not use all capitals for brand names like TOYOTA.

- Never write anything in an email that you would not write in a letter or memo. Foolish words may return to you!

Adapted from Hambridge (1995)

Section summary

> Select the means of communication based on the contents and choose the best method for the level of expression and complexity. Carefully design your email from the subject line to the closing to get the right content to your audience in the right way.

7

NEGOTIATION TACTICS

Tactics at the table

This chapter contains a few points about tactics used at the negotiating table. Tactics refers to actions you take during negotiation.

False concessions

It is not uncommon to offer a false concession, allowing the other party to struggle to get something that you would give them anyway. Your HIT list, discussed in Chapter 4, includes things you have to get. It might also include things you have to get rid of. If your "have to get" list includes something you must get rid of, it might be possible to trade it for a concession, as if you wanted to keep it. See the following example of a false concession (sometimes these are called "padded concessions").

Let's say that in the course of negotiations, Mr. A [of AMPO] demands in no uncertain terms that Commissioner Daniels be dismissed. Ms. C [of City] protests equally strenuously that her side will never agree to such a move. This is a strategic misrepresentation: City indeed wants to get rid of Daniels, but AMPO doesn't know it. Ms. C later "reluctantly" backs down . . . and gets Mr. A to make some concessions in addition.

The Art and Science of Negotiation, Raiffa, p. 142

Comment:
Please notice that "strategic misrepresentation" is a polite way to say "lie". This tactic is usually only effective in gaining small improvements and may

> damage the overall relationship. It is best not to lie, but it is also important not to give something for nothing. In this example, Ms. C perhaps could have openly given away the Commissioner and gained improved relationship without misrepresenting her position.

False concessions are not uncommon, so you should be aware of them. Avoid giving something for a false concession. Make false concessions carefully. If you offer a false concession, you must never reveal that you were planning to give it anyway!

Higher authority

Sometimes a negotiator will refuse to agree to a proposal that is entirely possible. In order to get more concessions, the negotiator might insist on getting approval from the boss. This negotiator may go out of the room and pretend to call the boss, hoping it will seem like it is not possible to give a small concession. In this situation, it is best to wait.

Trading information

The other side seeks information about your business activities and plans while asking about theirs. Allow the counterparties to lead the conversation if they want to. When asked, you should provide information as long as it is not sensitive or secret. The ideas about trading information are included in more detail in the section on reciprocity.

What information is too sensitive to share? That depends on your opinion. You may decide that it is OK to reveal all details (FOTE or Full Open and Truthful Exchange) or that some details should be kept secret, such as your reserve price (POTE or Partial Open and Truthful Exchange).

Silence

With some individuals, and even some cultures, silence feels uncomfortable at the negotiating table. If one side feels uncomfortable with silence, it may be possible to get a concession simply by looking thoughtful. Example: "How about $10,000?" (no answer) "Well, then $9,000?" In this example, the silent party does not need to give a concession in order to get a concession. While it may be effective, it is not a helpful tactic for building relationships and trust.

Experienced negotiators will not drop their price; instead, they will wait or ask questions in order to understand what the silent party can agree to.

FIGURE 7.1 The silent rejection tactic

Stalling

It is quite common to create a little extra time for your own thinking during a negotiation by asking for details or explanations that might not be really necessary. This kind of delay is called stalling. Generally negotiators understand and are comfortable with a little bit of stalling as one party or another thinks and plans. However, it is not considered acceptable to intentionally expend large amounts of time hoping to pressure another party into acting unwisely at the last moment.

If the counterparty stalls a lot, you should be prepared for them to give you sudden, complex offers shortly before the deadline for finishing the negotiation. You should be prepared to say no, to extend your negotiating time and to use your BATNA. You can use the time in which the other side is stalling to learn about them through questioning and other research methods. As time runs out, you should resist the pressure to agree. Instead, it may be possible to ask to work with another negotiator, possibly even moving up the hierarchy to work with the boss of the negotiator.

Another response is to move your schedule forward and inform the other team that you have very little time remaining, thus putting the same pressure on them. This is a hardball approach and not advised, just as extreme stalling is not advised. Last-minute decisions and agreements may contain significant errors and result in agreements that are poor for one or all parties, or that lead to expensive renegotiation or collapse.

In the past, US businesses, seeking to quickly close a deal, have been easy victims of stalling and have agreed to unfavorable terms shortly before leaving to the airport. However, smart US businesses are ready to quickly change partners or to allow much extra time for concluding negotiations.

If you choose to stall, you should be aware that the other side might use its BATNA and break off negotiations.

Last-minute demands

Some negotiators will make a request for a concession very late in the process, even as documents are prepared for signing. This tactic intends to catch the other side off guard or off balance, with the hope of getting an easy concession. The best reaction is not to agree immediately, but instead to make it clear that you have the time and willingness to renegotiate the entire package and all the related linked issues. Some negotiators will ask for a concession even after signing. The best reaction is not to agree immediately, but instead to make it clear that you have the time and willingness to renegotiate the entire package and all the related linked issues. You may, however, grant the extra concession. Why? Because it could help to build a relationship. In some regions, including Japan, a negotiation party may expect to give or expect to request "a little" in the comfortable belief that business partners can do a little extra if they are serious about the relationship.

Playing the hard card first

Some negotiators like to start with an aggressive stance even though they plan to be flexible and even soft during the negotiations. This is sometimes called playing the hard card. This tactic is a kind of impression management (see previous discussion in Chapter 2).

> Why would a negotiator do this? Write what you think are the advantages of playing the hard card first.
>
> _____
> _____
> _____

What kind of negotiators would be most likely to play the hard card when starting negotiations?

1. Male	6. From a little known company
2. Female	7. From a dominant culture
3. Experienced	8. From a subordinate culture
4. Inexperienced	9. Respected
5. From a well known company	10. With no reputation

If you chose the even numbered selections from the previous list, you would usually be right. These negotiators may feel it necessary to start with an aggressive approach because of their own insecurity. Handle these individuals by listening carefully and working through their concerns while showing respect for them and their offers. If a person fitting the odd numbered selections plays the hard card first, you may be wise to consider finding a different partner, whether in that company or in a competitor company. Switching to a person who uses more constructive and synergistic approaches may lead to improved mutual gains.

TABLE 7.1 Playing the hard card first

Party A: First of all, I want to let you know that we have cancelled several contracts similar to your proposal because they were not profitable enough.	Comment: Party A tries to show that they are tough negotiators. They hope to decrease Party B's expectations about results.
Possible response from Party B: I see. Maybe we should improve our offer to accommodate you.	Here, Party B seems to be impacted by this approach.
Possible response from Party B: I see. Well, we have a great product and offer, so let's talk about how we are better than those other companies.	In this response, Party B shows no impact and changes the focus of the aggressive opening to good qualities of the offer.

Why might a negotiator not play the hard card first? Write what you think are the disadvantages of playing the hard card first.

Negative or aggressive starts

A very aggressive or negative start may immediately lead to a similar negative response. As we know from the prisoner's dilemma game mentioned in Chapter 2, it is most common (and wise) to punish aggressive or other negative behavior by returning the same. The most likely series of events are shown in Figure 7.2.

In short, a negative move provides no incentive for a positive response. Therefore, it is generally best to avoid negative behavior throughout a negotiation.

Retracting an offer

Many people consider it unreasonable or even unethical to retract an offer after making it. But is it so bad? An offer is not an agreement. And a whole agreement is not finished until all the parts have been completed and formalized. On the other hand, if people generally do not expect offers to be retracted, someone who does it regularly may be socially ill – pathological. However, behaviors that seem very wrong among one group of people may seem quite acceptable in another group.

How would you feel if an offer was retracted a day or two after having agreed to it during negotiations?

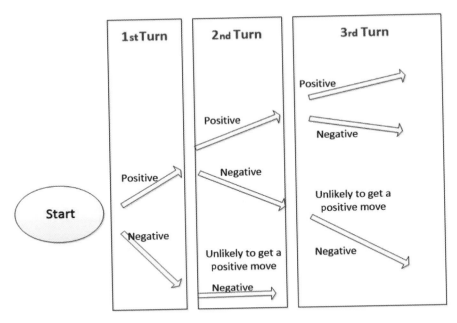

FIGURE 7.2 Start sour or sweet?

One person famous for retracting offers and other aggressive negotiation tactics was Steve Jobs, founder and sometime CEO of Apple. A Sony executive commenting in W. Isaacson's 2011 biography of Steve Jobs had this to say about Jobs:

> "'In classic Steve fashion, he would agree to something, but it would never happen," said Lack. "He would set you up and then pull it off the table. He's pathological, which can be useful in negotiations."
>
> (Isaacson, 2011, p. 401)

Job's success at business negotiation and his belligerent behavior are well known. Does that make it a best practice for Apple? For all companies? Write your thoughts here: _____

_____

What are some reasons not to retract an offer after it has been made?

_____

_____

_____

What are some reasons to retract an offer after it has been made?

_____

_____

_____

The result for Jobs and Sony was that they did agree to a deal, but only after much time and with fewer of the joint benefits than they might have received. Jobs' behavior alienated and upset his counterparty. The negotiations almost broke down. If another party had revealed similar technology, Apple might have lost the chance to get the Sony music.

Disinformation stratagem

The following quote is from Howard Raiffa's 2002 book on negotiation. He describes a disinformation tactic that he punished, but which is of course in use in the real world:

> One student, let me call him X, playing against Y, excused himself to go to the bathroom and left behind his written confidential instructions. Y couldn't resist noticing X's confidential RV and took advantage of X. Or so Y thought. Y did not know that X . . . put in a false number. Y lost mightily and X was triumphant. Y complained to the instructor of the unfair practices of X. The instructor docked points from both.
>
> (Raiffa, 2002, p. 271)

Of course, in a real world negotiation, there is no professor to enforce fairness or ethical behavior. Clearly it is ethically unacceptable to trick a business negotiation partner. In fact, if the result is very bad for one side, they may be able in some legal systems to annul the resulting contract legally if the trick is discovered. Even if there is no court proceeding, discovery of the tactic will probably damage the reputation of the party that managed the trickery. In addition, there may be the cost of lost time and money, as a contract broken or terminated must be replaced using other partners.

Ultimatums

An ultimatum is an aggressive offer usually like this one: "Accept the offer by 1 PM, or we are finished." An ultimatum usually damages the relationship and the negotiations in general. Avoid making ultimatums. Avoid reacting quickly to ultimatums.

Case: EuroDisney

In a widely discussed business case, Disney started an amusement park in France near Paris. The park had a disappointing start with low visitors and numerous difficulties. After some years, Disney found itself in severe financial trouble. They needed to renegotiate and restructure their debt burden, but the banks were not interested in negotiating.

Boldly, Disney informed the banks that they would have to negotiate or Disney would default and abandon the park, leaving the banks with a huge, unpaid, expensive and nearly useless property. The banks came to the table. Eventually all sides agreed to easier repayment terms, the Disney operation is still in business and the bank loans were paid.

Based on the case study, was Disney's ultimatum successful?

What did Disney's ultimatum demand?

Explain why it was or was not an acceptable hardball tactic.

How to manage an ultimatum

If another party gives you an ultimatum, please follow these guidelines:

- do not react quickly, even though there is pressure to react quickly;
- play for a little time (see Chapter 6 for useful phrases);
- coolly compare the ultimatum to your BATNA;
- ... walk away from the negotiation if necessary.

Play for longer time:

- propose value creating ideas;
- make counteroffers;
- link existing ideas and goals to the ultimatum.

Trashing the product (buyer tactic)

Sometimes a buyer will attack the product that is at the heart of a sale. The purpose is to show that the buyer is only barely willing to accept the product and therefore the price must come down to their estimation. The process of trashing the product can be quite long and thorough, particularly in negotiations with Chinese teams. An individual famous for starting negotiations with extensive trashing of the other parties' products was Steve Jobs, the founder and CEO of Apple.

Less experienced teams, especially from Western cultures, have found themselves shocked, upset, bored and irritated after listening to this process for hours or days. However, the best response to this process is to quietly listen, learn if possible how to better satisfy the customer and not give more than a symbolic concession. Therefore, you should have some symbolic concession prepared in advance. The worst way to react is to get upset or lower the price significantly.

Detecting lies and reacting to lies

It is generally wise to check for lies and deception, though without showing mistrust for the other parties. Cellich and Jain (2004) suggest following these three strategies to catch a lie.

1. Test the consistency of the other party's statements by comparing statements and by asking questions to confirm accurate information. This process is also called the "inconsistency trap". However, an inconsistent negotiator may not be trying to deceive. The negotiator may not be aware of the inconsistency – in such cases the "inconsistency trap" can help to clarify logical errors to the benefit of all parties.
2. Communicate in several ways (speaking, writing, email, fax, etc.) because it is harder to lie consistently in numerous formats. When speaking face-to-face, look for non-verbal cues such as gestures and eye and facial movements that reveal nervousness and possible deception.
3. Ask for tangible proof of issues that are in question (regulations, legal agreements, previous contracts).

If you think the other party is lying, you can follow one of these strategies.

*   React with silence until the other side clarifies the issues (not helpful if the other party does not understand why you are silent).
*   Express concern politely about the possible lie and wait for the other party to clarify it suitably.
*   Review your BATNA and decide if you should end the negotiation – it is unwise to work with a party that might lie.
*   Increase your efforts to learn about the other party and their interests.

Why you should not lie

You should not lie because:

*   if discovered, the relationship will be badly damaged;
*   a contract made based on a lie (or other fraud) can be voided in many legal systems including UNIDROIT, an international contract law accepted and enforced in many countries. After voiding the contract due to a mistake based

on a lie, the liar may have to pay damages according to UNIDROIT (Art. 3.2(2), UNIDROIT Principles, 2010);

- your reputation among other businesses may decline.

What to do if the other party . . .

- . . . wants a price too high or low for you: ask questions about the specific points they expect. Break down the costs item by item. See if you can add or remove expensive or unnecessary items.
- . . . delivers a final demand or request (an ultimatum) that you dislike such as "this is my last offer": don't accept or reject it immediately. Gain time and information by asking more detailed questions about the offer. If this is a fixed BATNA position, you may have to choose to agree or to leave the negotiation. If it is not a fixed point, the other side will eventually allow some concessions or cooperation.
- . . . offers a great price at the beginning: do not immediately accept it, even if it is good. Learn more about it so that you can either improve the price or develop a more complex and valuable business relationship with the other party.
- . . . uses a "sad song" to play on emotions: this tactic makes a heartfelt request for significant concessions. In North America or Europe, a sad song might come at the beginning or middle of negotiations – pay no attention to it. In some parts of the world, the sad song may require some sympathetic reaction including perhaps minor concessions. However, do not give large concessions for it. In Japan this tactic (called *naniwabushi*) is sometimes used successfully against non-Japanese companies that do not expect or understand it, though research done for this textbook suggests it is less common than in the past. Ignoring the sad song and giving nothing may damage the relationship – it may be part of cementing the relationship for some organizations in some cultures.

Discuss with your partners: which of the previous tactics are hardball? Which are soft? Medium? Do you think people from different countries might have different answers?

Avoiding unethical negotiation tactics

Please review this useful article by Roger Dawson on identifying and avoiding unethical tactics:

http://reiclub.com/articles/real%20estate%20negotiating.

Defense against the dark arts: age and experience

With time, you will learn to quickly identify aggressive tactics as they happen. You will simply become more sensitive to tactics. When you identify the tactic, you will know how best to react. Generally, the best reactions combine further communication and managing the relationship. But do not change your position because of the tactic – only change your position based on negotiated concessions and joint problem solving.

In many cases, your most powerful defense against aggressive negotiation tactics will be time. The more time you have, the more flexibly, carefully and constructively you can react during the negotiation. Make it clear to all parties (your boss, the other negotiation parties, your co-workers and other important stakeholders) that you need and will use as much time as necessary to get a result that maximizes gains for all sides.

Section summary

> Use all tactics carefully – these are essentially not frank negotiation approaches. Avoid hardball negotiation tactics and the people who use them.
> The key defense against all negative tactics is to keep a cool head and work patiently forward based on the mutual interests of the parties.

Case: The very emotional client

Real life is a complicated and messy thing. Your plans may not last long after making contact with the other sides in a negotiation. Flexibility is the answer! In the following case, we will see how a negotiation party acted and reacted to the behavior of another party at the table. This example, from the experience of a construction industry manager in Alberta, Canada, shows how one party reconsidered and redesigned its goals, strategy and tactics as the interaction progressed. At the same time, another party in the negotiation redefined their role radically. The third party in the negotiation did not react flexibly and had to collapse in the end.

Background

This project was difficult from the beginning. It was a hard-bid, small TI project in a shopping mall with a very short schedule. We (the construction company) ended up with some poor suppliers and had to work long hours and nights to meet the schedule. The client also made some changes during the course of our work. With ten days to go, we realized we were going to miss the deadline by four days. Our management and consulting team were made aware of this, and the client planned accordingly. Meanwhile, the millworker was put on notice and was to be held accountable for costs incurred as he was at fault for the delays.

Issue

After the client moved in, he made us aware that he was going to charge us for lost earnings for the four days. We disagreed with him, as there was no penalty clause in the contract and he had made the changes that delayed the project. Because we worked with the consultant a lot (high importance of relationship) and the millworker was responsible for the costs, we wanted to try to negotiate a compromise. We asked the client for a written claim of damages; however, the client avoided us and delayed providing the costs. Normally, we would have placed a lien against the project, but we couldn't due to the fact that it was in a mall. After 46 days, we received a claim from the client in the amount exactly equal to the holdback fee (10 percent of the agreed project fee), including notice that he had no intention of releasing the holdback.

First negotiation

Our walk-away was 3 percent, as this is what the millworker offered us to make this problem go away. So this was offered to the client to avoid further negotiations or legal options. It was rejected. The client had no interest in budging on his Win/Lose perspective. Our compromise strategy changed to a competition tactic due to the negotiation style of the client ("competition").

Our position

Our new target was zero percent loss, as we were quite protected by the contract. We were aware that the client and his agent (the consultant) did not communicate well, and that the consultant was sloppy at reviewing paperwork.

Second negotiation

The client started the meeting very emotionally, stating that by opening four days late, we ruined his reputation and cost him exorbitant profit. Our team was well prepared and did not get personal or emotional. Our first question was "Please provide documentation supporting your claim." He refused, stating that he didn't have to provide this because his gut told him this was the correct amount, and he came to this number from all his years of experience. We disagreed and explained that he needed to prove his number or we would move to legal options, as his "gut" would not be supported by the court (we were confident to use a threat as our tactic, because our documentation exceeded his). He got very frustrated and aggressive. The consultant called for a quick break to advise their client. After the break, the client agreed to provide supporting documentation.

We thanked him for changing his position. At that point, we asked the client why we were meeting – from our review of all documentation, we were not late but actually one month early. This stopped all conversation for a minute or so. The consultant spoke up, asking us to clarify this because we missed the contract date by four days. We responded by pointing out that there were numerous changes to the project, we added time to each change order and the consultant signed them. There was conversation between the consultant and the client. They produced four approved change orders, totaling a three-day extension. The client then argued that all of his losses happened on the fourth day, and that if we had completed the project within the three days, he would not be looking for damages.

We then reminded the client that we had another change order approved that added 30 days to the contract. This caused lots of commotion as the consultant could not find the change order. The PM produced the signed paperwork proving our claim. The client was raging at us and his consultant, specifically when he realized that the change order was approved a couple of days before the original contract completion date. We responded by stating that contract law supported us, and we expected to be paid in full. The client sat in his chair with a very defeated look on his face, and the consultant called for a break. After the break, the consultant stated that they were willing to negotiate and accept our original offer of 3 percent. We declined and stated that we would seek an alternate dispute resolution (ADR) or legal means to collect all outstanding monies. We agreed to park the issue and end the meeting.

We soon received a call from the consultant stating that the client agreed with our position, mostly. It was made clear that the client needed a token to release payment, or he would find other ways to drag out payment including the legitimacy of the approved change orders. Satisfied that a small token would end this and we would receive payment, we offered 1 percent to the client and it was accepted. We then got an agreement with the millworker to cover this cost, which he was glad to do as it was less than his first offer (3 percent). We were quickly paid by the client, just 24 hours later.

Source: Used with permission, Penn, 2013.

Questions for discussion

Was the negotiator able to strengthen their BATNA against the Emotional Client?

_____

_____

What role did the Consultant play in this negotiation?

_____

_____

What were some of the errors of the Emotional Client?

_____

_____

How well did the negotiator know the Consultant?

_____

_____

In Figure 7.4, we can see that the first round of the negotiation put the client and consultant in a position against the constructor. As the negotiation moved into the

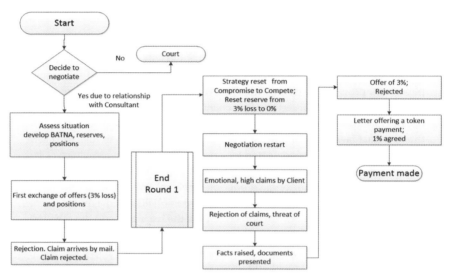

FIGURE 7.3 Flow chart of the emotional client

TABLE 7.2 Interests table for the case of the emotional client

Party	Issue 1	Issue 2	Issue 3
Client			
Constructor			
Consultant			

TABLE 7.3 Stakeholder analysis table for the case of the emotional client

	Rights	Responsibilities	Wants	Needs	Comment
Client					
Constructor					
Consultant					

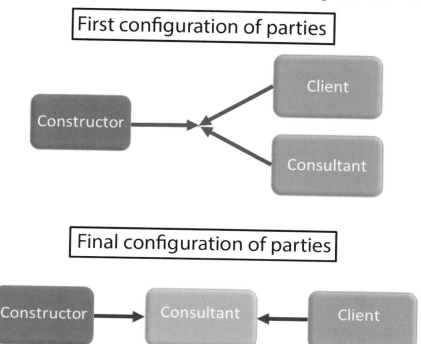

FIGURE 7.4 How the roles changed

second round, the consultant stopped supporting the client and moved to a position where he could support both sides somewhat in order to mediate the conflict toward a successful end. The consultant showed insight and flexibility in changing position.

Persuasion approaches

Negotiators can use several approaches to influence the thinking of the other sides. Li and Sadler (2011) summarize nine varieties of influence strategies, several of which we will discuss here.

Legitimating

This approach may be effective with parties that place high importance on relative rank and prestige of individuals and organizations. The legitimating approach links proposals to respected people and institutions to increase the respect for the proposal. For example, the proposing side may point out that the proposal is similar to the work of a famous person familiar to the other parties. Suggesting that your proposal has been accepted in the past by a business leader such as Bill Gates might influence the other side to accept it. To be effective, the choice of legitimating person or organization must match well with the knowledge and thinking of the other parties.

Rational persuasion

This approach relies on thinking that seems logical and sensible to the other parties. Presenting data about industry standards or the expectations of people in a certain region may help a party agree to a proposal that is in line with that data. One example could be offering salaries that are 5 percent better than the local standard instead of paying each individual according to their specific merits. This approach may be most effective with negotiators who are rational in style as described in Chapter 9.

Inspirational appeals

This approach relies on transmitting emotional involvement and commitment to the other parties. Showing how a proposal would benefit a large number of people or a specific group might make the proposal more appealing. For example, a member of an ethnic minority may be swayed by a proposal that benefits other members of that community. This approach may be effective with parties that have a strong sense of community and collective action (see the comment on *guanxi* in Chapter 6).

Ingratiation

This approach is a way to build relationships; however, it is insincere. Flattery may be effective in the short term, however long term relationships are best when built on mutual success and satisfaction. Ingratiation is a process to urge the other sides into positive thinking before asking for high demands that they might not otherwise accept.

Strategic exchange

This approach refers back to previous interactions when one side has made concessions and would now like the other parties to make concessions. This persuasive tactic can only work where there is a strong relationship that has survived several transactions and will probably continue to survive for many more. If the party receiving the strategic exchange proposal does not foresee a long-term positive relationship, it will have no motivation to agree.

Other approaches described by Li and Sadler include coercive threats (discussed in Chapter 6 of this textbook), as well as jointly consulting to solve problems (discussed in several places in this textbook).

Section summary

> Use various approaches to persuasion depending on the nature of the situation and what you know about the counterparty.

Humor in the negotiation

Appropriate humor has at least three useful functions in a negotiation:

- to decrease tension;
- to build rapport;
- to devalue a proposal.

In a negotiation, you can use humor carefully to relax the groups. At the same time, humor builds rapport and positive feeling among the negotiating parties and can be used systematically to manage the relationship (Vuorela, 2005). Humor therefore has a similar positive effect and value as small talk. Humor requires the participation of all parties to be successful, so it is fundamentally cooperative (Vuorela, 2005). Any jokes should be easy to understand, simple and only gently distracting. Jokes that distract too much from the atmosphere and the topic will seem unprofessional and will not build rapport.

Devaluing a proposal

Read the example and give your reaction to the question:

> His negotiation partner had suggested a much higher dollar allocation for sand. The first negotiator responded:
> "Yeah, we need to get some sand, but we're not trying to build Malibu Beach here, man."
>
> (Halpern and McLean, 1993, p. 62)

What do you think the second negotiator felt when hearing this response?

Used this way, humor is a tactic that can make a proposal you want to reject seem bad to all parties. Careful and gentle use of humor like this can make a proposal seem weak without damaging the relationship. Slightly stronger use of such humor may seem mocking and will probably damage the relationship. Here is an example of devaluing humor and the result as reported in an academic journal.

As an example, one of the male participants did not want to spend a lot of money on sand for ground cover. His negotiation partner had suggested a much higher dollar allocation for sand. The first negotiator responded:

"Yeah, we need to get some sand, but we're not trying to build Malibu Beach here, man."

With this joke, he made the other negotiator's request for more sand look ridiculous. They ordered less sand.

Halpern and McLean, 1993, p. 62.

Inappropriate humor will damage the relationship, and the joke-making side can lose status and seem foolish. Generally speaking, inappropriate humor includes complicated jokes (including satiric and ironic content), jokes on taboo or sensitive subjects and anything that could seem insulting. Of course, please do not tell jokes as if a comedian had joined the negotiating team!

Revealing issues through humor

In her work on humor in negotiation, Joan Emerson (1969) found that a joking reference to a difficult or even taboo problem could help identify and address an issue to other parties. Because an issue might be unacceptable in a serious conversation, it might be acceptable in a joking context. That in turn could allow the topic to be handled seriously.

Example of poorly executed humor:

Party A: You know, this reminds me of the time I was in a bar and doctor and a horse walked in. Party B: A horse? Party A: Yeah, and the horse says, "Give me a beer and a gallon of water." Party: Who said that? Party A: Well, it is a joke, you see . . . Party B: Oh. Let's consider the cost in your proposal . . .	In this example Party B has not even identified the statement as a joke. This means that Party A has tried the joke at the wrong time or has not introduced it properly. As a result, Party B may consider the other person to be foolish or wasteful of time.

Example of well executed humor to decrease tension:

> *Extract One: Client Negotiation*
> 1   SellerJ   So we in the U.K. we've got about just
> 2   (SIPS COFFEE)
> 3   round about seventy people working for
>   the company **we've got**
> 4   **forty-two service engineers running
>   about in little white vans [an'**
> 5   **things like that**
> 6   BuyerM   **right ha**

Reprinted with permission, Vuorela, 2005, p. 112

Vuorela holds that this humor-based approach strengthens feelings of joint purpose in some negotiations.

Section summary

> Humor is a useful tool to build relationships and send signals about offers. However, it must be used carefully with sensitivity toward language skills and face saving issues.

Ethics

Do no harm

Your negotiating should always focus on building value for your company and your projects. At the same time, you should actively try to not hurt the other side when sharing existing or future value. Actively means that you review the agreements and the processes before completing the negotiations. This is quite different than passively allowing the other parties to make mistakes that are part of (or not part of) the business being negotiated.

Q: Why should I spend the time and effort to check that the other side is OK?
A: Because being part of a negotiation with a bad outcome for the counterparties will directly harm them and indirectly harm you. In the same way that you would help a person avoid an accident on the street, as a businessperson, you are expected to help others avoid damaging errors.
Of course, if your negotiating partner comes to harm, others may suspect you of harming them and the result may be damage to your reputation. Whether you are or are not guilty of harming the other party, damage to your reputation may occur – therefore, it is best for you to actively prevent damage to your reputation by helping your negotiation partners avoid damaging errors.
Additionally, if your negotiating results are too hard for the other parties to manage, they may:

- go out of business;
- feel forced to break an agreement;
- refuse to do business with you in the future;
- try to renegotiate the agreement.

Any of these results means additional cost and lost time to you.

Example

Company A managed a hard bargain against company B to supply memory chips. Company B agreed to a very low price, just a little more than their costs. Suddenly, a new regulation caused one of their inputs to become more expensive, and they were forced into bankruptcy. Company A suddenly found itself with no supplier, as well as an urgent need to find a new partner and make a new agreement. In the months spent searching and negotiating, they lost market share, income and the faith of their customers.

Help others build value

You should help the other parties in a negotiation build value in activities you are not interested in.

Q: Why should I help some company make money when it does not include my company, especially if it is not even my business area?

    A1: Because you will benefit from the improved relationship between the two companies.

    A2: Directing the other parties towards good business ideas will not prevent you from getting full value out of the negotiations.

    A3: You may be able to build a more robust agreement that will not collapse or need to be renegotiated if there is an economic downturn or if unexpected problems arise. That could save you money and time.

Case: Ethics makes money for Honest Tea and CapriSun

Honest Tea, a drinks maker, searched for a way to reuse the packages from their kids' drinks. They found none. Finally they found a recycler that could use the drink package (a pouch) in some fabrics . . . but what to make? In 2007, Terracycle suggested bags and kids' backpacks. The backpacks carry the name of the recycler and Honest Tea (good for corporate image), but Honest Tea takes no profit from the bags. The recycler, however, is able to grow a reliable business that serves Honest Tea. See www.terracycle.net for more products.

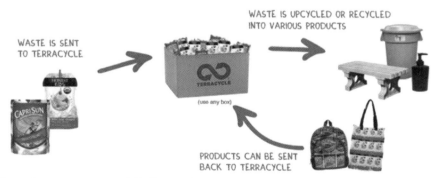

Recycle your waste with Capri Sun® and Honest Kids®

FIGURE 7.5 Honest Tea, Capri Sun, and Terracycle joint recycling solution

Source: Image used with permission of Terracycle.

This ethical approach also benefitted CapriSun, a maker of drinks for kids and competitor of Honest Tea. CapriSun joined the Terracycle pouch recycling program in 2008. The previous case supports the idea that ethics can contribute to the strength of your company. Ethical business behavior is not just a cost.

Be ethical, but get all the value you can

Your ethical actions neither prevent you from getting more value than the other side nor from taking value that the other side does not recognize, seek or care about.

Example

Let's remember Tanba Agro and Hyogo Cake. The cake factory finally agreed to buy the eggs. Consider their next conversation.

Traditional view:
ethics are just another cost

Gross income	¥100,000
Ethics	¥-15,000
Insurance	¥-8,000
Maintenance	¥-10,000
Taxes	¥-6,000
Net income	¥61,000

New view:
ethics can contribute to income

Gross income	¥100,000
Ethics	¥15,000
Insurance	¥-8,000
Maintenance	¥-10,000
Taxes	¥-6,000
Net income	¥91,000

FIGURE 7.6 Ethics as a net gain

TABLE 7.4 Ethics in action

Dialog	Comment
Tanba Agro: By the way, do you want us to take away the eggshells? Hyogo Cake: What? We usually throw them out. Tanba Agro: That is 100kg of trash everyday. We can pick them up a little cheaper than the cost of the trash service. Hyogo Cake: OK!	Tanba can use the eggs as a source of calcium for the chickens. They will save money by taking the eggshells. They have agreed to get a valuable item (eggshells) from Hyogo for free.

In your opinion, is there an ethical problem in the previous conversation or not?

Business negotiator's oath of ethics

I will not actively harm another person or company with the process or results of negotiating. I will actively check that the other parties in a negotiation are not harmed by their or my actions or agreements.

Section summary

> Be sure not to harm other companies, organizations or people intentionally or unintentionally as a result of your negotiating.

Who should you *not* negotiate with?

There are some companies and organizations you should avoid – they may cheat, even if the agreement is robust. Use your BATNA, because deals with them are bad or very risky. Learn about organizations you should avoid by reading and by talking to people with more experience. Try to get positive references about an organization before starting negotiations.

Generally avoid companies that:

1. have a reputation for very aggressive agreements and hardball tactics;
    a. Some big car companies, for example, are excessively demanding with suppliers regarding price, delivery schedule, response time, exclusivity, etc.
    b. Some large retailers force prices down to the level of minimal profit, making it hard for the supplier to survive.
2. have a history of fraud or legal problems;
    a. Some companies have transferred intellectual property or secret business information to other companies or governments. Don't give those organizations the opportunity to sell your secrets! Even working with organizations like that may damage your reputation.
    b. Some companies have many ongoing disagreements about contracts. They may frequently be in court, arbitration or in settlement actions. Do research to find partners who have a history of completing contracts with few legal disputes.
    c. Some countries regularly rule against foreign companies when there is a problem – avoid doing business with organizations in those countries.
3. engage in unethical/illegal behaviors.
    a. Some companies mistreat their workers in their home country or in other countries.
    b. Some companies have frequently made low quality or unsafe products.
    c. Some companies may want to negotiate with competitors to set prices within the industry (see news article http://www.nytimes.com/2013/09/27/business/9-auto-parts-makers-plead-guilty-to-fixing-prices.html?ref=business).

If you must negotiate with a company of this sort, be sure to have a strong BATNA. It may be better to use the BATNA before you start talking!

Why do the bad guys continue to conduct business and find partners? After decades of bad experiences, we would expect whole countries, not to mention companies, to be shunned. Yet new companies are attracted to them despite their bad reputation and record. The answers to this question seem to fall into these categories:

1. Extremely appealing terms are offered. Inexperienced businesspeople may be strongly attracted by the chance to grow profit margins. However, more experienced negotiators will recognize that the offer can seem very appealing, but the other side may never pay out fully.
2. Many businesses think they are smart enough not to get tricked – "It won't happen to us!"
3. Businesses may have no alternative due to a weak BATNA or monopoly situation.
4. Social/political pressure requires dealing with a bad partner, at a loss, in order to gain other profitable opportunities.

Section summary

Avoid negotiations (and close partnerships) with organizations that could hurt your business or your reputation.

8
WIN AT HOME BEFORE YOU GO

Educating the boss and coworkers

Teach your coworkers, superiors and staff about negotiation so they can help you, and additionally so they can understand your results.

Proper support

You know that a negotiator needs time and information to prepare for a negotiation. The people who work with you may not know that. They may not understand how much information you need to have. They may not understand why you need to think the way your negotiation counterparties think. Without understanding and support at home, you may not get the support necessary to be successful.

After a negotiation, you will always need to explain why the deal you got was good. You might explain to your boss, your coworkers, the board of directors or others. If they do not understand negotiation, they may not understand your results. Explain key concepts to them.

Questions

What points and what terminology should you teach your coworkers and other management staff regarding negotiation?

List some points that you feel are necessary, but not too difficult to teach.

1. _____	5. _____
2. _____	6. _____
3. _____	7. _____
4. _____	8. _____

Section summary

> Educate your boss and coworkers to gain their support and understanding before and after the negotiation. You will not improve the long-term success of your company if you are the only good negotiator in it!

Back table negotiations

In your working life, negotiation tasks will generally start with requirements from your boss. A simplified negotiation task might be, "Don't spend more than $X, get these concessions, and finish it by Friday next week." Notice that this sort of task assignment is lacking even enough information to complete the HIT list discussed in Chapter 4.

As a negotiator, you have to understand and satisfy your back table. In the end, you will have to explain to that person or group why you agreed to the deal you got. You can also indirectly communicate to the back table of other parties. An Austrian business owner interviewed for this book said he always gave economic reasons for his offers that the other party could take to their boss. A Japanese business owner in Tokyo described in an interview how she explains advantages for the other side based on her knowledge of their bosses and companies.

Case: Fuji Seiko activity

> Consider this case regarding Fuji Seiko.
> You have offered the Fuji Seiko negotiation team the following terms, but you know they have to report the offers to headquarters for approval. Your product is a little better than your competitors, but a little more expensive. How would you help the Fuji Seiko team win the argument with their bosses?
> Terms:
>
> - three partial payments instead of one lump sum;
> - delivery one week earlier;
> - adjustment of color to match the Fuji Seiko product.
>
> Example argument:
> Let your CFO know that we will accept three payments with no price increase – it may help with cash flow.
>
> Your arguments:
> _____
> _____
> _____

_____

_____

Write one or two reasons why you should consider the back tables of other parties in a negotiation.

_____

_____

_____

_____

The back back table

Behind the back table, you may find the back back table, a spooky space inhabited by ghosts. These ghosts are people or organizations that you cannot communicate with, but that may have influence regarding your choice of outcomes or your negotiation process. Examples of these ghosts include retired or even deceased coworkers, company founders, idealized famous personalities, political figures and mythic business leaders.

As an example, the authors are aware of a Tokyo company that cannot divest itself of an underperforming US bank because its acquisition was by an executive manager whose importance in the company was closely tied to it. The executive has been retired for 15 years, yet the current directors will not even discuss selling the bank because it might insult that retired person. Even though that person no longer participates in the company, he blocks the discussion to restructure. His ghost at the table blocks any movement on the issue.

Ghosts such as the one described can:

- block topic areas from discussion (impose taboos);
- block outcomes even if they represent practical results;
- create a cognitive bias against logical problem solving.

Section summary

> Pay careful attention to your back table in order to move smoothly from talks to agreements. The back table must be satisfied with your negotiation results before a proper agreement can be made.

Problem solving techniques

Many experienced negotiators are good at problem solving. They think creatively, react flexibly, and they know useful tools and techniques. Some of these tools and an overall process are presented in this section.

An overall process for problem solving might start with a high-level analysis of people and facts, describe problems, identify root causes of problems and find possible solutions for discussion. The overall process should begin long before the negotiation parties meet. Later, however, the process should include all parties – doing so will boost communication and problem-solving power. The following sequence of steps is a good way to start. With some practice and experience, you might find a sequence of steps you prefer more.

Ishikawa diagram (fishbone)

An Ishikawa diagram is used to identify and categorize issues contributing to a problem. A useful diagram can be made quickly. Generally, these start with the categories shown in Figure 8.2: people, policies, equipment and environment. The

TABLE 8.1 Tools for problem solving

Step	Tool	Purpose
1	Stakeholder analysis	Establish the groups and individuals involved directly or indirectly, their level of power (the ability to influence decisions) and their needs and goals. See Appendix VI for further explanation.
2	Ishikawa diagram (fishbone)	Roughly sketch the issues contributing to a problem.
3	Why-why (five whys)	Determine causes and ultimately root causes of each issue.
4	What	Identify what to do and achieve in order to solve the problem.
5	How	Propose how to solve each problem.
6	Creative solutions	Expand the discussion from single problems to integrate related problems and solutions.

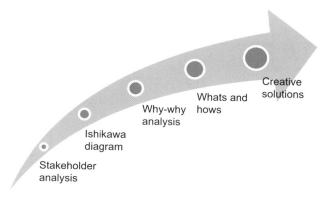

FIGURE 8.1 Sequence of analyses for problem solving

problem itself is written into the head of the fish (it is often called a fishbone diagram).

Figure 8.3 for a high speed rail line, based on a student's work, uses the four basic categories to find causes of complaints about quality of life by residents near the rail line.

The four categories, people, policies, equipment and environment, in the previous examples are just suggestions. They are a good starting point because they cover common problem areas. However, when working on a negotiation problem, start with these four but also replace and supplement them with other categories that are suitable for the problem you are working on.

Why-why (five whys)

After using the Ishikawa fishbone to identify the contributing problems, select one for better understanding. Drill down into the contributing problem to find a root cause using the "five whys" approach developed by Toyota Motor Corporation.

In the following example, the starting problem is the long wait that newly recruited staff experience before entering the standard training program – up to six months. Each time the why question has more than one answer, the diagram branches. Each of these answers may continue or branch until arriving at a root cause.

Notice that different branches may come to the same answers and root causes. Some branches finish sooner than others – so how can we know when to stop asking why? Analysts usually follow these guidelines:

- circular (points you back to a previous why in the same branch);
- no longer logically related to the original question;

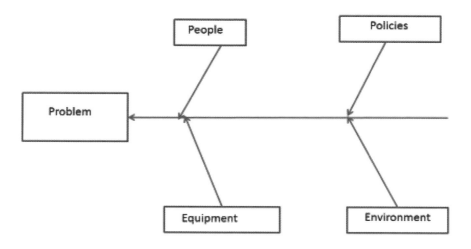

FIGURE 8.2 Ishikawa diagram, basic

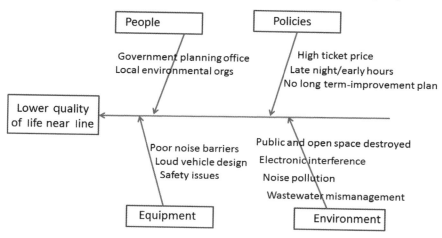

FIGURE 8.3 Ishikawa diagram, high-speed train line

- outside the range of the problem/organization;
- natural limits of physics.

Reviewing Figure 8.4 carefully, we can see that a lack of established procedures causes poor communication, which in turn causes the starting problem. Other root causes contribute as well. Figure 8.4 has provided a starting point, in fact several starting points, for fixing the original problem.

Looking at Figure 8.4, we can see that some answers are the same, but on different branches. It is common for different problems in the middle of the diagram to have the same intermediate cause. So a root cause might appear in more than one place. However, branches with the same intermediate causes should end with the same root cause or be explained in a note. The previous example is corrected in Figure 8.5.

Figure 8.5 now clearly shows the root causes, no matter where they appear, in white boxes. Some of the root causes appear to be the same, while others seem to have ended without a root cause (note the items in patterned boxes). An improved version appears as Figure 8.6, showing root causes including causes that merge at the ends of branches.

What/how

Now that the why-why has been completed with clear root causes, it is possible to add a What column at the edge of the why-why that shows what needs to be achieved.

The What column is an easy way to communicate the obvious needs for correcting the root causes of the starting problem. Additionally, Figure 8.7 communicates

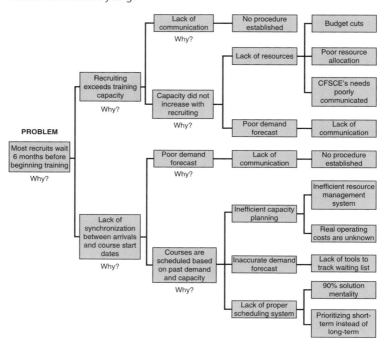

FIGURE 8.4 Five whys example

Source: Used with permission, Lavoie, 2013.

that some of the root causes require the same action. For ten root causes, we have eight fixes to undertake. And some that seemed the same on the surface need different fixes.

The next step is to add a How column at the edge after the what column to list how to achieve those items. This How column does not need to be detailed. It is a starting point for serious planning and joint work with the various partners in the negotiation.

Now that a rough set of problems and solutions exists, you can join forces with the other negotiation parties to work out the details while creating and claiming value in a well-informed process.

Creative solutions

During the first five steps in the process this textbook proposes, your team might work alone or with the negotiation partners. If there is an established, comfortable relationship, all steps can be done jointly. If not, the last step of the problem-solving sequence is the one where the parties must unavoidably join forces. But some might say, "Better to work on the solutions alone and be sure to get the best ones for yourself! Don't let the other parties join!"

What do you think? Please write down the advantages and disadvantages of working out the solutions without the negotiation counterparties.

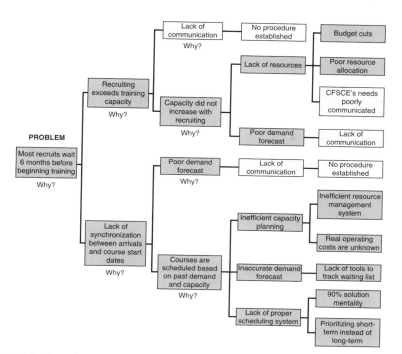

FIGURE 8.5 Five whys: roots not clear

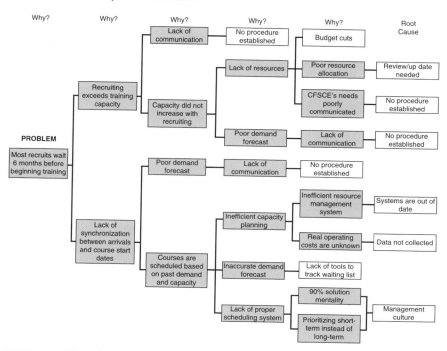

FIGURE 8.6 Five whys: roots clear

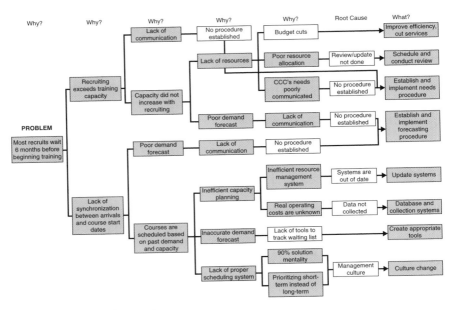

FIGURE 8.7 From why to what

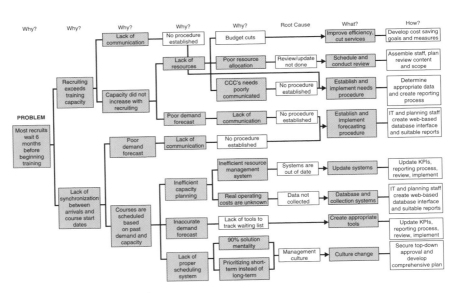

FIGURE 8.8 From what to how

Advantages of working on solutions alone	Disadvantages of working on solutions alone

If you consider the potential for improved ideas as well as the value of building satisfaction and relationships, and the possibility for building those things through frequent interaction over problem solving, you may see good reasons for sharing the solution-creating step and even most of the earlier steps.

Section summary

> Use these techniques (and other approaches) to solve problems both before the negotiation and during with the participation of all other sides.

War gaming as preparation

This textbook includes real and fictitious cases to use in learning how to prepare and execute negotiations. Some of the cases appear as games and role-playing opportunities. Why stop playing the negotiation game at the end of this course? In your future negotiations, the preparation team can take the roles of the counterparties in addition to their own real roles. As your team members represent the other sides, you will:

- learn how the other side thinks;
- gain understanding of their interests;
- identify matching interests;
- identify conflicting interests.

Simulating and modeling the negotiation will help you communicate with the counterparties, and help you discover how to create and claim value with them. This practice and discovery approach is sometimes called *war gaming*.

Red Team vs. Blue Team

Organizations facing high stakes negotiations sometimes make a team for each side, for example Red and Blue teams. The Red Team will play the roles of other organizations or individuals in the negotiation, with the Blue Team taking the "home" role. All teams work without contacting each other for an agreed period of time (days or weeks) to research interests, strategies, tactics and issues. When the teams meet again, they will behave as in a real negotiation, presenting offers and counteroffers, proposing solutions to problems and distributing resources as they see necessary.

Case: War gaming example

> Komsel, Inc. and Singcell, Pty. plan a difficult negotiation. They have many common interests, but resources are very limited. Komsel decides to conduct a war game in advance, hoping to identify the probable limits of Singcell in order to present their own ideas without unnecessary conflict.
>
> Komsel therefore selects staff members for a Red Team that will play the role of Singcell in a mock encounter. The Blue Team includes the Komsel staff members who will go into real negotiations with Singcell a few weeks later.

Some organizations will go so far as to hire actors who look and behave like the real counterparts on the other negotiating teams.

> Write down the advantages you see in a Red Team v. Blue Team war gaming practice:
>
> _____
>
> _____
>
> Write down the disadvantages you see:
>
> _____
>
> _____

Additional benefit – greater creativity

When the participants in a war gaming exercise include some of the actual negotiators, the war game can be used to explore broad possibilities. Dr. Larry Susskind (2013), writes that is becomes possible to consider ". . . a range of possible options that the parties might never discover under normal circumstances". The actual negotiation, if it is very tense, may not allow the negotiators to discuss options that would bring criticism from back table observers. However, putting the issues into an unofficial war game situation may provide the freedom to bring up, and seriously

TABLE 8.2 War gaming sheet, Komsel's Red Team representing Singcell

Red Team Members	Staff member from Komsel assigned to understand that role	Interests	Comments
CFO Legal counsel Senior engineer Other team member			

discuss, solutions that would otherwise be taboo. The advantage is that additional solutions get consideration and may be put into play in the real negotiations that follow.

Additional benefit – intuitive thinking

War gaming creates knowledge that is not easy to pass along and explain – we gain negotiation skills best through years of experience and interaction with highly skilled coworkers. This kind of knowledge, tacit knowledge, does not develop quickly or independently (Polyani, 1967; Nonaka and Takeuchi, 1995). However, time is a resource that may be in short supply. Even if we have years available, it may not be possible to gather suitable experience unless there are numerous challenging negotiations annually. Lastly, each major negotiation is likely to be unique, so how can we develop so much deeply intuitive knowledge quickly enough?

Share the knowledge and experiences gained from the simulated negotiation through in depth communication among the assembled team members. Through communicating, maximize discussion and reflection that leads to tacit knowledge in the individuals and in the team as a whole. Conducting the negotiation more than one time will increase gains in experience and uncover various possibilities to create and claim value.

The war gaming approach will help you and your team to develop the deep, unspoken and intuitive knowledge that will lead you and your staff to quick and sure action at the real event.

Section summary

Simulating a negotiation with your own staff playing the counterparties will help with understanding the possible interests and solutions. Further, you may improve team performance regarding speed and mutual understanding.

Financial modeling

When negotiating, make use of financial projections supported by spreadsheets and financial modeling software. These can include spreadsheets that you develop or models used in your organization. Oracle's CrystalBall software is a widely used general-purpose package of financial models that can be used to create financial projections. DecisionShare software from Integratto is particularly useful for assessing uncertain numbers such as the level of sales and costs or profits associated with a product or service. Without knowing the exact number of units that will be sold, profits and costs are similarly hard to establish. Additionally, DecisionShare helps to analyze, display and rank the importance and sensitivity of elements in a complex negotiation. For example, the software might reveal that a feature such as cost or estimates of sales or price point is of greatest impact. The parties can then agree on how to resolve the issue before it becomes a block to the negotiation. In addition to the tools mentioned, a variety of calculators and financial tools can be found on websites for free use.

Section summary

> When negotiation requires prediction of uncertain financial numbers, use software tools to simulate. Then choose the actions that will have the best results.

9

WHAT KIND OF NEGOTIATOR . . .

. . . are you? . . . are they?

How do you resolve disputes?

The Thomas–Kilmann Conflict Mode model is widely used to describe how conflict is resolved. The model compares how assertive a party is to how cooperative a party is regarding any issue. The model can be used to judge your own approach on any one issue or the approach of a counterparty to an issue. Figure 9.1 is very similar to the one presented in Figure 1.3 in Chapter 1. The key difference is that this one helps you to understand individual styles (yours and others) as you plan your negotiation.

The concepts in the model have the following meaning:

- competing – taking a distributive, Win/Lose approach without joint wins;
- avoiding – delaying or never discussing an issue;
- accommodating – accepting proposals of the other parties with little or no change;
- compromising – sharing some benefits and disadvantages among the parties;
- collaborating – working together on solutions and plans.

Note that collaborating falls short of creating synergy as discussed in Chapter 3, in the section on principle-based negotiation. Synergy means that completely new joint plans and value are created together.

Of course, your choices based on the previous chart will change depending on the issue and the context around the issue. However, you should be able to identify and understand your general preferences and the preferences of your counterparties.

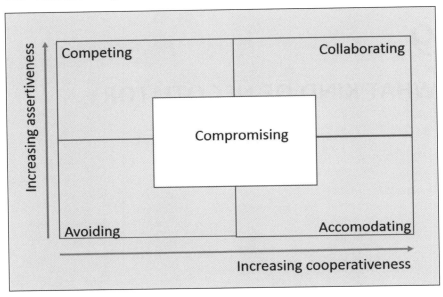

FIGURE 9.1 Thomas–Kilmann Conflict Mode Model

Source: Thomas and Kilmann, 2007.

Emotional style

Each person has an emotional style. Some are more relaxed, warm, insistent, empathic, introverted or extroverted. Knowing more about yourself, your team and your counterparts will help you adjust to their style and improve communication. Use the quiz in Figure 9.2 from Leigh Thompson's (2012) book, *The Mind and Heart of the Negotiator*, to learn more about your emotional style.

In the quiz, "R" means rational, "P" means positive and "N" means negative. Based on your score and your preferences, you can choose to continue without change or to adjust your style.

> Rational – preference for less emotional content, preference for more logic.
> Positive – preference for relationship.
> Negative – preference for competition and winning.

Emotional intelligence

Emotional Intelligence (EQ) is the ability to correctly identify and understand the feelings of others (Bessert, 2007). Knowing those feelings makes it more possible to find solutions that your negotiation partners will accept.

To learn more about EQ, take an online quiz like the one at http://www.ihhp.com/free-eq-quiz/ or http://greatergood.berkeley.edu/ei_quiz/. You can learn

Read each statement, and indicate whether you think it is true or false for you in a negotiation situation. Force yourself to answer each one as generally true or false (i.e., do not respond with "I don't know").

1. In a negotiation situation, it is best to "keep a cool head."
2. I believe that in negotiations you can "catch more flies with honey."
3. It is important to me that I maintain control in a negotiation situation.
4. Establishing a positive sense of rapport with the other party is key to effective negotiation.
5. I am good at displaying emotions in negotiation to get what I want.
6. Emotions are the downfall of effective negotiation.
7. I definitely believe that the "squeaky wheel gets the grease" in many negotiation situations.
8. If you are nice in negotiations, you can get more than if you are cold or neutral.
9. In negotiation, you have to "fight fire with fire."
10. I honestly think better when I am in a good mood.
11. I would never want to let the other party know how I really felt in a negotiation.
12. I believe that in negotiations you can "catch more flies with a flyswatter."
13. I have used emotion to manipulate others in negotiations.
14. I believe that good moods are definitely contagious.
15. It is very important to make a very positive first impression when negotiating.
16. The downfall of many negotiators is that they lose personal control in a negotiation.
17. It is best to keep a "poker face" in negotiation situations.
18. It is very important to get the other person to respect you when negotiating.
19. I definitely want to leave the negotiation with the other party feeling good.
20. If the other party gets emotional, you can use it to your advantage in a negotiation.
21. I believe that it is important to "get on the same wavelength" as the other party.
22. It is important to demonstrate "resolve" in a negotiation.
23. If I sensed that I was not under control, I would call a temporary halt to the negotiation.
24. I would not hesitate to make a threat in a negotiation situation if I felt the other party would believe it.

Scoring Yourself

Computing your "R" score: Look at items #1, #3, #6, #11, #16, #17, #20, #23. Give yourself 1 point for every "true" answer and subtract 1 point for every "false" answer. Then combine your scores for your R score (rational).

Computing your "P" score: Look at items #2, #4, #8, #10, #14, #15, #19, #21. Give yourself 1 point for every "true" answer and subtract 1 point for every "false" answer. Then combine your scores for your P score (positive).

Computing your "N" score: Look at items #5, #7, #9, #12, #13, #18, #22, #24. Give yourself 1 point for every "true" answer and subtract 1 point for every "false" answer. Then combine your scores for your N score (negative).

FIGURE 9.2 Emotional style questionnaire

Reprinted with permission, Thompson, 2012, p. 117.

more about personalities in order to evaluate yourself, your team members and the other negotiating parties using the five factor model, the Myers Briggs Type Inventory (MBTI) or other approaches.

Comparing

It is possible to compare individuals based on their styles. Figure 9.3, for example, compares two people based on their styles including rational, negative, positive, assertive and EQ.

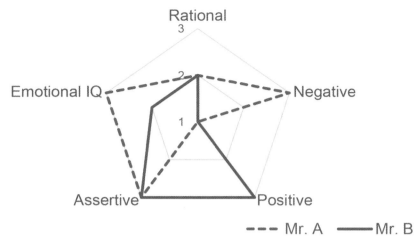

FIGURE 9.3 Personal styles compared

To create a radar map like the previous one, measure the five characteristics broadly and simply as high, medium and low with scores of three, two and one respectively. The advantages of comparing individuals are explained in the following text box.

Knowing the style of counterparties will help you know what to expect from them.

- Rational parties may avoid showing emotions and may react poorly to displays of emotion.
- Negative parties may manipulate by displaying emotions and may escalate emotions that they perceive in others.
- Positive parties may seek to build relationships and be sensitive to positive emotions.

Knowing the style of counterparties will help you to adjust to them.

- Rational parties may react well to proposals based on logic and fairness.
- Negative parties may react well to proposals in which they perceive extra benefit, a win, for themselves.
- Positive parties may react well to proposals that show improvements in relationships.

Knowing the style of counterparties will help you to manage them.

- Rational parties may be managed by showing logical steps and conclusions.
- Negative parties may be managed by avoiding a competitive spiral.
- Positive parties may be managed by including the value of relationship in offers.

Source: Thompson (2012, p. 116), Chapter 5

Assertive

Assertive teammates may reinforce each other's assertiveness. Weakly assertive individuals may find that together they are more effective at putting their ideas into the conversation. On the other hand, strongly assertive teammates may become overpowering, smothering ideas that could come from other parties.

Section summary

Learn about yourself and your counterparties in order to best manage your approaches and the behaviors of the counterparties.

Cognitive bias

Understanding yourself as a negotiator also means you must understand how you think. The term "cognitive bias" means influences on thinking that can lead to errors. These errors are important to understand and avoid because they may lead to poor decision making. There are many kinds of cognitive bias — some that are of interest to negotiators are described further.

Example of framing

A small tech company, Zing, Inc., is entering negotiations with a large, well-known globalized electronics maker, Pineapple Corp.

Section summary

Good business thinking is not always strictly logical. However, try to identify and avoid bias in your thinking that could lead to mistakes.

Bias and decision making

The ideal decision making process is one that is conducted in multiple steps, without time pressure, by experienced people. When time and resources are limited, the process is often compressed or shortened, with poor decision making as a result. Even under the best conditions, the decision makers can fall into cognitive bias.

The process previously described may have good results. In a business negotiation, the process can be done by one side, or jointly with other sides if the relationship has developed strongly. Mutual problem solving will lead to mutual satisfaction and mutual gains. However, time is not always available for a slow and careful decision making process.

TABLE 9.1 Types and impacts of cognitive bias

Type of bias	Explanation	Negotiation impact (examples)
Anchoring	Starting with a high sale price or low purchase price can create a bias that shifts the entire price discussion to move within a limited range.	Anchoring is effective if the other parties are not familiar with the concept and do not re-anchor. If another party anchors far from your target, simply re-anchor in the opposite direction in order to neutralize their anchor.
Confirmation/ expectation Bias	Interpreting data based on what you expect it to be, for example expecting winter to be cold and wearing a coat even on a warm day.	Thinking that the other sides are friendly and not reacting appropriately when they show unfriendly behaviors.
Emotional bias	Sympathy or distaste for a person, team or topic may impact decisions.	Negotiators may make agreements that do not optimize gains or cooperation.
Framing	Overall presentation of an issue or idea (e.g. positive/ negative; urgent/non-urgent; important/less important).	Expressing a problem as "a chance to work together on solutions" is much more positive than presenting it as a difficulty. Research (Neale and Bazerman, 1985) shows that positive framing leads to higher mutual gains than negative framing.
Law of small numbers (representativeness)	A small sample is inappropriately interpreted as widely true (Tversky and Kahnemann, 1971).	A negotiator must insist on high quality data (i.e. new, clearly explained, detailed and not aggregated) and must interpret that data carefully. Skills in statistics are appropriate and negotiators should take the time, even if inconvenient, to understand data.
Optimism/ Overconfidence	Expecting to gain more than is likely. Research (Neale and Bazerman, 1985) shows that negotiators who expect to gain are less likely to make concessions and make agreements.	Negotiators may feel dissatisfaction despite a good agreement, raising the expectations of the back table unreasonably.
Prejudice	Failing to take new information into account because of existing ideas about the subject.	Rejecting the solutions proposed by certain people because your culture expects those people to have poor business thinking.

Type of bias	Explanation	Negotiation impact (examples)
Undervaluing bias	Concessions are not evaluated accurately; instead, they are evaluated lower than their real worth.	Because the receiving party often undervalues concessions, it is useful to make numerous small concessions rather than a single large one.
Vivid information bias	Responding too strongly to data that are striking (Nisbitt and Ross, 1980). Example: we may be afraid of flying because air accidents are front-page news involving large numbers of people. In fact, however, air travel is much safer than road travel by most measures.	Skilled negotiators must not overvalue shocking or surprising points of information.

TABLE 9.2 Framing and reframing

Version 1	Version 2
Thank you so much for taking the time to consider our xZhei technology. We hope you will find it suitable for your projects!	So, I understand you are interested in our xZhei technology.
This version creates a mindset that the large company is doing the small one a favor.	This version creates a mindset that the small company holds something that the large company wants.

High pressure, high speed process for negotiators

Negotiators in the midst of negotiations may feel high pressure to act and decide quickly regarding complex issues and solutions. The pressure may come from their back table, the counterparties, external sources or their own feelings about the negotiation. In situations like this, the negotiators may shorten the process. Below is one way to manage a shortened process. Note that this shorter process can only be successful if the negotiators have identified the problem and have prepared alternative solutions, at least partly, in advance. It is important for the negotiators to resist time pressure and evaluate offers slowly and thoroughly.

1. Compare offer to alternatives prepared in advance →
2. Review for bias →
3. Select best →
4. Discuss amendments internally and with counterparties →
5. Accept or refine →
6. Agree to implementation with options to refine or change.

TABLE 9.3 Decision making process and bias

Process	Bias
Identify the problem → Make an intuitive judgment and set it aside → Gather information → Analyze the problem and solution parameters → Evaluate → Create solutions → Predict results of solutions → Compare solutions and your intuitive judgment → Select best → Implement best solution → Evaluate results → Adjust the decision or implementation based on the evaluation.	Many kinds of bias can enter the process at any stage. Therefore, review and consideration of bias should be conducted throughout the process.

Note that the process described above allows for intuition. Take this step early to improve your intuitive abilities and to capture the input of team members, especially those with lots of experience. Very experienced people are often able to correctly decide about complex situations quickly because of their years of modeling, practice and observation (Kahneman, 2011). Writing down the intuitive solutions and comparing them to more deliberate solutions will:

a. identify situations that are particularly difficult and which need more work;
b. build up the skills of less experienced staff members.

In the ideal process presented earlier, careful decision makers review for bias throughout all the steps. In the shortened practical process, the negotiators should add a specific step to consider bias. In this step, they can identify bias and propose changes to the solution, or reject it completely, in order to avoid a poor decision. The shortened version also requires negotiators to have some alternative scenarios prepared in advance – do your homework!

Kepner-Tregoe decision making process

This widely used process is described in the seminal book *The New Rational Manager*. The "rational process" the authors propose follows four steps: situational appraisal, problem analysis, decision analysis and potential problem analysis (Kepner and Tregoe, 1997).

Those steps include stating the decision to be made, developing objectives on a must versus must not and want versus avoid basis, weighting the wanted results, creating alternative solutions and screening the alternatives to arrive at a final best possible choice (Parker and Mosely, 2008). It is important to understand that this model does not start with proposing solutions and trying to pick the best one – that approach may lead to time wasting efforts that do not take the desired outcomes into consideration. The steps might appear as follows.

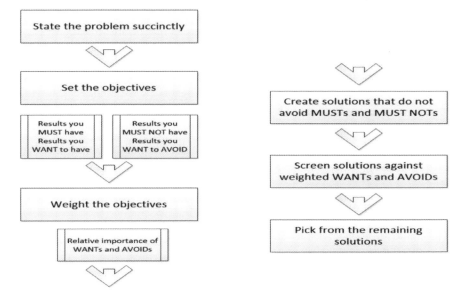

FIGURE 9.4 Steps in Kepner–Tregoe model

Pluses and minuses of Kepner–Tregoe model:

+ starts with clearly identifying the decision to be made;
+ clarifies objectives into must/must not and want/avoid;
+ understanding the must/must not and want/avoid helps avoid taking on useless data;
+ screening process to avoid a poor choice.

However:

− fails to address bias as a discreet step or parallel process.

Section summary

> Look for cognitive bias in your ideas, and try to avoid bad decisions based these errors.
>
> Practice your decision making process with your team.

Teamwork

On a soccer team, there are players who specialize in defending or attacking. However, even specialized players must always defend and attack as necessary – the roles must overlap. A negotiation team can work similarly. Some team members can specialize regarding certain issues, but all members should be able to support each other in practical ways.

Unlike soccer, small teams are generally best in negotiation, unless there are many very complex topics. Generally a negotiation team should have one or two specialists or technical people, a knowledgeable generalist and a decision maker (usually a manager authorized to make certain decisions). The actions of the team members must overlap as they support each other. The team may have many members, but they do not all have to go to the negotiation table. Similarly, the members of a negotiation team work together by:

a. having special roles;
b. supporting each other in all roles.

The following suggested roles are for teams at the table (during planning, teams may take different structures as convenient).

Leader:

* Agrees to agenda;
* Keeps agenda on track;
* Acts to resolve or avoid deadlock;
* Agrees to final proposal;
* Supports specialists when they are leading the conversation.

Specialist:

* Leads the conversation when those special topics are in discussion;
* Agrees to a specific point when your criteria are met (or signals leader to agree);
* Supports leader and other specialists when they are leading the conversation.

Q: What does it mean to support other team members?
A: It means you must carefully follow the talking and your team's overall plan. If you notice a problem, an opportunity, a mistake, new information, etc., you need to communicate it to your team members. You can do this by:

* silently writing a brief note and passing it to other team members;
* quietly and briefly speaking to a team member;
* directly speaking to the counterparty about it.

This kind of communication is called supportive interaction (Vuorela, 2005). Vuorela gives these examples:

* "The sellers ensure that all their arguments are covered with the help of teamwork, with different members of the team contributing to the on-going discussion at different times" (p. 29).

- "They also take turns at times repeating an argument a co-team member put forth earlier, and sometimes this seems enough to convince the buyers of their argument" (p. 29).

Q: Is teamwork good for getting all arguments and opinions out openly?

A: Yes. "Teamwork is a useful tool in covering the 'full front' when pursuing an argument with every member of the sales team bringing forth a different angle of the argument" (Vuorela, 2005, p. 80). For example, if the conversation moves to another topic before all the key points have been discussed, a team member can carefully interrupt and return to the unfinished topic. Teams that have members who are skeptical or disruptive of the agreement gain the benefit of dealing with hard challenges. These challenges may help the team avoid errors in the agreement.

Q: Is it OK to talk with your team members during a negotiation?

A: Generally you should use some internal talk, but avoid talking too much because it will distract others. You can put in a word or brief comment or question if your team is used to this behavior. Also, you can talk with your teammates loudly and clearly in a way that the counterparties can join. However, internal conferences with long whispering are generally poor etiquette. If you need a conference with your team, politely ask the other side to give you a few minutes of privacy or propose a general break for refreshments. Use the break time to coordinate with your teammates.

Using notepaper or tablet devices to communicate internally is effective, and not very distracting to teammates and counterparties. Be sure that your teammates can comfortably use such methods by practicing before trying it at the negotiating table.

Q: What is "team building"?

A: It means becoming good at working together. This happens by practicing and discussing strategies and details together in depth. A team leader needs strong listening skills in order to understand the individual members, identify the skills and strengths of the team and attempt to make weak areas stronger. At the same time, the team leader needs to understand the goals of the individuals in order to align them with the goals of the team and the company. In addition to frequent meetings (one-to-one and as a group), having a casual meal or drinks together helps to build team function. If the team is created specifically for the negotiation, it may be possible to select compatible team members based on their personalities and skills.

Teams need frequent interaction and communication in order to share their knowledge effectively. The sharing of knowledge builds up tacit knowledge (Polyani, 1966; Nonaka and Takeuchi, 1995) and intuitive capacity. With time, teams can become very fast to act and decide. See the section on war gaming in Chapter 8 for comments on building the ability of a team to work well together.

Read the descriptions of these teams and decide with your partner which is best.

TABLE 9.4 Preferred team size and composition

Team A includes	Team B includes
Two engineers with appropriate specializations	One engineer
One marketing person	One marketing manager
Two business managers	One business manager
One top level manager (CEO, COO, GM or other)	
One note taker	
One finance person	
One human resources person	

Please fill out the following:

I think Team _____ is best because . . .

_____

_____

_____

Intercultural teams

Teams that include people from various cultures face some challenges and enjoy some advantages.

Write some possible disadvantages here:

_____

_____

_____

Write some possible advantages here:

_____

_____

_____

One of the most commonly identified difficulties with intercultural teams is the increased time for communication that is necessary to get the same results. Inexperienced managers may be surprised by lack of progress as deadlines approach. Frequent one-to-one communication may help to establish the relationships and mutual confidence necessary for a team to work well together.

Teams that are spread across many locations and meet mainly online or by phone may experience difficulties such as time coordination, miscommunication, lack of clarity about tasks, delays and so on. Consider the individual's personality and culture carefully, as some will appreciate additional communication, while others will find it upsetting. Adjust the mixture of voice, email and other media to suit the individuals.

When considering the members of an intercultural team, the team leader might aim to gather people with similar rank, previous positive intercultural experience and reasonably strong skills in a common language.

Common language within the team

The common language of business is usually English, although other languages are dominant such as Chinese in much of East Asia or French, Spanish, Turkish and Arabic in other regions. A team that includes native and non-native speakers will need the native speakers to help improve their comprehension, for example by using less slang, a slower speed, careful pronunciation and simple grammar choices. At the same time, the non-native speakers may need to concentrate on their own pronunciation, choice of phrases and ability to ask for clarification. Gestures and use of pauses, facial expressions and humor will also need adjustment – mutually, not by one group or person only. See Browaeys and Price (2011), *Understanding Cross-Cultural Management*, chapters 15–17, for additional useful comments on these topics.

Section summary

Make sure your team understands the goals, the plan and all of the steps well. Practice together, prepare together and communicate frequently.

10
FINAL PHASE

Robust agreements that can survive

At the negotiating table, you should end with clear written agreements that your legal team will later finalize. You hope that these agreements will survive as intended.

How can you make an agreement that the other parties will not reconsider and perhaps break? How can you make a robust agreement, even in a country that has a poor legal system? How can you get cooperation from people who are distracted with other projects?

Your ideas:

_____

_____

_____

These approaches may help:

1. Include short-term incentives to continue.
2. Plan actions in steps or milestones that must be completed and accepted before continuing.
3. Include negative outcomes to deter breaking off.
4. Share value fairly.
5. Communicate the value creation of continuing.
6. Plan for "predictable surprises".
7. Communicate to be sure the other sides understand the benefit of joint cooperation.

8. Create contingent agreements that change with the circumstances in a way that all sides consider fair.
9. Communicate the high probability of additional successful work in the future or, even better, agree to future projects that follow up on the current project (build the relationship, cement the relationship).

The last item on the list first came up at the beginning of this textbook. It is part of all good negotiation thinking from start to finish. This is the easiest, most obvious, most effective way to increase the likelihood of cooperation and minimize the chance of breaking off or cheating.

Movius and Susskind (2009) write, "Design nearly self enforcing agreements." That means agreements that reward completion through incentives and make non-completion unappealing through punishments or claw backs.

Dr. Larry Susskind (2013) of MIT suggests making agreements that help against "predictable" surprises. We know that even good ships sink, so we put lifeboats on them. Even good agreements may be harmed by a bad economy, changes in regulation or other "surprises" that we can reasonably expect. Create agreements that can survive such surprises.

Case: The agreement that needed renegotiation

Starbucks, the café chain, found itself in an agreement it could not live with. After a strong start selling coffee products with Kraft in 1998, the environment changed. But there was no date for ending or reviewing the agreement. Starbucks felt in 2010 that it was necessary to bring the agreement to an end, and offered Kraft cash to end the agreement. Kraft, however, refused. Thereafter Starbucks simply broke the agreement. Kraft insisted on arbitration, which it won in 2013.

As noted in the Harvard Law School article at <bit.ly/1tyCV56>, the companies could have and should have agreed to a time or set of conditions for renegotiation. Writing these issues out would have provided an easy and cheap process for continuing, changing or terminating the agreement.

In the end, both parties wasted money and decision-making time. Starbucks additionally had to pay all the profits it made on similar coffee products after breaking the agreement, over $1 billion, to the Kraft spin-off company, Mondelez.

Section summary

Design agreements that can survive changes in the environment.

Control mechanisms often found in negotiated agreements

After the deal has been agreed upon and the discussion has finished, how can you be sure that the other sides will do as agreed? There are many ways to control the actions of negotiation parties after the talking has finished. These can be summarized as follows:

- provide reasons (incentives) for the other sides to complete the work in a satisfactory way;
- provide reasons (disincentives) for the other parties not do incomplete, late or unsatisfactory work.

Some of the mechanisms for giving those incentives and disincentives are described as follows.

Milestones: Agreed intermediate points of completion. When each milestone is reached, payments and new commitments are made. In a joint venture for manufacturing, milestones might include purchasing a factory site, installing utility services, constructing the building, installing equipment and so on. Each major step is a milestone and an incentive to continue. The opposite would be an agreement that simply describes a single completed target.

Example:

"Upon completion of the Working Prototype detailed in Section 3 of this agreement, Party A will pay Party B $900,000 by bank transfer within five working days."

Gates: Points in a project when resources are re-allocated. An agreement with gates allows the parties to commit resources when necessary and suitable instead of committing major resources years in advance. The advantages include flexibility and the ability to withdraw if a project fails.

Example:

"After completion and acceptance of Phase 3 of the contract, the parties agree to discuss allocation of resources for Phase 5, including the following points ..."

Incentives: Reasons, usually financial, for a party to perform above the minimum required in an agreement. For example, a party that completes a task a week in advance might receive 5 percent more in payment.

Example:

"Completion of installation of the equipment more than five working days in advance of the schedule set out in Paragraph 7 of this contract will entitle party A to an additional payment of 5 percent by Party B within the payment terms of Paragraph 12 of this contract."

Claw back: An agreement to return part or all of a payment if a task is not done as required.

Example:

"In agreement with Section 17a of this document, Party A will pay Party B $10,000 in order to cover startup costs associated with the project. Should the target of $80,000 gross sales not be reached by 31 November, Party A reserves the right to insist that Party B repay 75 percent of the $10,000 startup costs paid by Party A, totaling $7,500."

Punishments and penalties: The opposite of incentives. Typical punishments include receiving less payment if a task is completed late or with low quality.

Example:

"Party A will receive only 90 percent of the sum in Section 7b if the polishing work is not completed within 30 business days after the date of the agreement of this contract."

Contingent clauses: These are built in "if" structures.

Example:

"Party A will conduct the E17 test procedure if Party B is unable to complete development of the substrate by 17 December 2016."

Renegotiation clauses: If conditions change, the parties can return to a negotiation instead of facing a drastically unbalanced business situation. In this way, both parties can avoid situations that could be very destructive of their business and avoid the need to unilaterally break the agreement.

Example:

The parties shall reconvene to discuss Section 3 of this agreement should the price of gold decrease below $1100 for longer than one week.

Renewal clauses: These allow the parties to continue business if a major change to a product is made such as a new edition of software or a reference book.

Example:

In the case that Party A updates the Software Product, they will inform Party B in advance of the update. Party B will have the first opportunity to agree to continue or renegotiate the current agreement within five working days of receiving notification from Party A.

And of course. . . don't pay fully in advance!

Section summary

> Create good agreements that encourage success through fair sharing, incentives, communication and high likelihood of future activities. Use control mechanisms that all sides agree are fair in order to encourage the parties to proactively solve problems and avoid difficulties.

When agreements don't survive: outside support, mediation and arbitration

Negotiation does not always result in great agreements and satisfied partners. If the agreements are poorly designed, with gaps in understanding, no enforcement mechanisms and no tools to repair a disagreement, the partners may want to renegotiate some or all of the agreement. That of course costs more time, money and energy. . . so it is better to develop good agreements in the first place!

When to renegotiate

You can expect your business partners to renegotiate an agreement if some or any of the following conditions exist:

- a drastic change in the economic environment occurs;
- availability of resources changes;
- new regulations or legislation impacts the business activity;
- political atmosphere changes;
- disasters or wars occur;
- renegotiation is part of the culture or personality of a party;
- relationship considerations change with respect to economic needs.

In some cultures and companies, renegotiation is considered a bad outcome – a failure. In other places however, renegotiation is seen as a way to expand the relationship and the business activity.

In any case, renegotiating part or all of an agreement is better than allowing the agreement to collapse. Recall the case of Starbucks and Kraft discussed previously. It would have been most sensible for Starbucks to have renegotiated before breaking the agreement. In fact, their failure to renegotiate and their failure to honor the agreement cost them more than the profits earned by breaking the agreement.

What if the parties cannot come to terms despite trying to renegotiate, and the agreement collapses? It may be time to call in a third party that will act as a neutral helper.

Process facilitators, mediators and consultants

Facilitators, mediators and consultants are paid outsiders, usually negotiation professionals, hired to move negotiations along. Usually they are selected by mutual agreement among the negotiating parties because they are experienced, respected and trained. They may regulate the flow of discussion like a traffic police officer regulates a busy intersection – they may ensure the negotiation process is fair or certify that information is correct by accessing confidential information on all sides. They usually do not deal with deeply substantive issues, however they help the parties voice their views, actively listen to each other and can help the parties create solutions through use of problem-solving techniques.

Mediation, facilitation and consulting are generally done with careful regard for neutrality. Even though these professionals are normally hired by mutual agreement as neutral outsiders, they will emphasize their neutrality in various ways, for example by sitting in the middle of the parties, not with one group or another. Additionally, they may offer confidential conversations with one or all sides in order to better understand the thinking, positions and goals of the parties. A careful observer will understand that a mediator or facilitator can never be truly neutral or impartial – participation in the problems and parties is what makes a mediator effective. A useful overview of mediation, including a general set of rules, can be found on the website of the World Intellectual Property Organization (n.d.).

Buddhist mediation

Buddhist mediators attempt to facilitate resolution of disputes by applying Buddhist practices such as:

- awareness of self (mindfulness). Mindfulness refers to keeping overall awareness of multiple facts, positions, opinions, etc. as objects in the mind, including one's personal thoughts and feelings, as objects separate from the self or the situation. Mindfulness supports attention (Burke, 2010), analysis, comprehension and the creative development of solutions (Ostafin and Kassman, 2012).
- separation of self from the emotions, pressures and statements of the problem. Separation allows the individual not to become attached to positions, events, feelings, demands, personalities and so on. No longer attached to a specific issue or detail, the parties can evaluate their goals and the goals of other parties more objectively.
- awareness of interdependencies. Parties learn that the best solutions are ones that include the participation and satisfaction of all sides to the greatest extent possible. Without interdependent action and resolution, it is very like that one or more parties will reject the results immediately or later.

- awareness of options for problem solving. As the previous processes develop, the parties, including the mediator, become more easily able to create solutions that may have been perceived as impossible, taboo or unattainable before. Even very unlikely proposals may provide elements that appear in the ultimate solution.

These practices are explained and taught to the mediation parties as necessary when the mediation begins and throughout the process.

While these approaches may be appropriate in areas with strongly Buddhist cultures, they may also be welcomed in North America and Europe. Some approaches that have been used among Buddhist mediators in the English-speaking world include (Kramarae, 2013):

- understanding-based mediation approach;
- insight mediation framework;
- nonviolent communication (NVC) framework;
- consensus making framework.

Islamic mediation

Mediation in the Islamic world is based on Sharia, the system of laws stemming from Koranic teaching. The term *wasaata* is widely used, and the process focuses on gaining an outcome that will bring disputing parties to a peaceful resolution. The *wasaata* process is intended to include comprehensiveness and flexibility (Bouhera-oua, 2008), especially through the mediator's fairness, appropriate knowledge and possible intervention. Furthermore, the *wasaata* process involves the wider community, whereas mediation and arbitration in the European and North American tradition are usually limited to the immediate participants (Pely, 2011). Ideally, the mediation includes reconciliation (*sulha*) in order to bring about a state in which the parties are expected to have no further disagreement or bad feeling. *Wasaata* is not a process specifically for business, though business disputes may be managed by a *wasaata – sulha* process.

External experts and fact-finders

Experts and fact-finders may be asked to help when the negotiators lack the knowledge, time or skill to investigate a question fully. In some cases, a third party may be brought in from another organization, a consulting company, a university, government or a competitor to provide information in a neutral and objective way. The negotiators expect that additional data and neutral interpretations will help them to find solutions – external experts and fact-finders are usually not included in the negotiation process and do not directly participate in problem solving. Ideally, fact-finding processes should happen early in the negotiation process, however in reality, they are often only started when the parties have run into a block because they need more information.

Ombudsperson

The ombudsperson (sometimes called an ombudsman) is found inside an organization and may be useful if your negotiation is internal to that organization (for example in the context of labor negotiations). Their job is to make sure that the process of negotiating an internal disagreement is fair. They seek to resolve problems early before they involve higher levels of management and more resources. The ombudsperson is relatively independent despite being inside the organization. The neutrality of the ombudsperson is usually not in question because they do not make binding decisions – they only help the parties to understand. The ombudsperson might, however, propose resolutions to the parties in a dispute as well as to upper level management in order to help the organization avoid similar problems in the future.

Disputes: arbitration or court

Arbitration is, at its core, not a negotiation process. It is a formal process for resolving a dispute and binding the parties to solutions. After arbitration, the relationship between the parties may be too damaged to re-engage in new business projects. Therefore, it is better to try negotiation, mediation and all the supports mentioned previously before going to arbitration.

Because arbitration is a formal process, it is more expensive than negotiation or mediation, though less expensive than a legal court.

1. The parties to arbitration agree in advance to accept the ruling and the solution of the arbitrator.
2. The parties agree to an arbitrator or a team of arbitrators that they view as neutral.
3. The parties and arbitrators agree to a process, usually with rules about presenting documents, arguments and counterarguments.
4. The parties prepare and submit documents and summaries of their positions.
5. Usually there is a face-to-face verbal discussion.
6. After the discussion, usually weeks or months later, the arbitrators will deliver a decision that is legally binding.

Section summary

> When negotiations fail or become deadlocked, use alternative methods to restart the process. Agreeing through negotiation, however, will usually be the least formal and least expensive way to reach agreements.

Draft agreements

Draft agreements can be made at the table. Draft agreements indicate intent, and the parties may agree that they are not binding until legal counsel draws up final agreements. On the other hand, a binding agreement can be made at the negotiating table if the parties wish. Negotiators who prefer detailed complex legal agreements will not feel comfortable with a binding agreement completed at the table – they will prefer to have a final version completed later by legal staff.

Draft agreements can be general or specific. Some individuals and some cultures will prefer more or less detailed documents. Generally speaking, Anglo-American cultures prefer detailed agreements and negotiations. The written documents, draft or final, can be many pages in length.

A detailed agreement should cover at least the following items:

- compliance
- confidentiality
- contributions from all parties
- damages
- dispute resolution
- enforcement
- exclusivity (including sector, channel, territory, etc.)
- force majeure
- improved versions, new editions, etc.
- infringement
- liability
- organizational structure/ownership
- parties
- purpose
- payment terms (e.g. in advance, upon completion, by milestone or other payment structures)
- representations, warranties and covenants
- risk (e.g. inflation risk, currency risk, political risk, etc.)
- share of profits/compensation
- tasks for implementation, obligations
- term (length of time the agreement will continue)
- termination
- transfer of obligation
- units of measurement
- waivers

Other cultures, especially Latin, Pacific, and East Asian cultures, often prefer general agreements that show intent and broad commitment. These documents may be quite short, even just a few pages. As an example, the author's part time contract with a university in Japan filled barely two pages. A similar agreement with a university in Canada filled 16 pages!

This textbook, however, recommends detailed agreements in order to minimize opportunities for misunderstanding and dispute. Well-designed agreements can save time and cost over the long term. The following sections list some agreement documents that you might work with.

Memorandum of Understanding (MOU) or Letter of Intent (LOI)

An MOU or LOI is usually not written with high detail. It is usually not legally binding. The purpose of the document is to describe the spirit of a cooperative agreement and broadly how the cooperation will function.

Contract

A contract is highly structured and is binding once the legal representatives of the organizations have signed it. A contract might contain the following sections, as noted in Bradlow and Finkelstein (2013).

- Recitals – identifies the companies and substance of the agreement.
- Definitions – defines words, especially technical jargon used.
- Business terms – core issues of who, what, where, when, cost, etc.
- Representations and warranties – statements of fact, such as "the factory at 33 Maple St. can support equipment weighing up to two tons per square meter."
- Covenants and agreements – generally these are promises to perform.
- Conditions – these include conditions that must be met, such as inspections, before the agreement comes into force.
- Indemnification – liabilities from failure to perform the covenants and agreements.
- Miscellaneous – may include clauses about termination, renegotiation and so on.
- Attachments and schedules – these may include lists of equipment, facilities, staff, property or other materials important to the agreement.

Agreement text examples

For examples of texts (free or for fee) that can be used in agreements, please visit some of the following websites:

General

> http://www.wipo.int
> http://www.lawmart.com

Dispute resolution

> http://www.jamsadr.com
> http://www.iccwbo.org
> http://www.huschblackwell.com

Confidentiality

> http://www.bitlaw.com/forms/nda.html
> http://www.hbs.edu/entrepreneurship/pdf/Sample_NDA.pdf

Section summary

Create agreements that cover details to the satisfaction of all parties. Agree to create draft agreements that are non-binding to allow time for review by legal professionals.

11
REVIEW FROM A HIGH ALTITUDE

What is the overall thinking and approach, the heart and mind of negotiation we need to follow? Lax and Sebenius (2006, p. 253) say "Think strategically, act opportunistically". To do so, they suggest the following strategic approach:

- Assess set up barriers:
  - Thoroughly map all the parties, their interests and their BATNAs.
  - Decide sequence and process.
- Assess barriers to agreement.
- Assess tactical and interpersonal barriers.
- Overcome these barriers by mapping backward from the target deal by making a 3D Strategy:
  - Set up the right negotiation content and goals.
  - Design value-creating possibilities.
  - Emphasize problem solving as a joint approach.

                    Adapted from *3D Negotiation*, Lax and Sebenius, p. 237.

Acting opportunistically means being flexible and ready to change your ideas in order to get the best results.

> Only effective preparation and focused action make the difference – and in our experience, the best preparation is mastering the principles of 3D Negotiation.
>
> (*3D Negotiation*, Lax and Sebenius, p. 19)

Your goal: "create and claim value for the long term."

(*3D Negotiation*, Lax and Sebenius, p. 237)

Another way of thinking about the overall goal and purpose of business negotiation is to think, "Let's maximize value, solve problems and avoid failure." Maximizing value means putting new value creation before distribution of resources and rewards. Solving problems means creatively removing barriers to agreement and developing value-creating ideas. Avoiding failure means designing agreements that are workable, enforceable and profitable.

An overall process is shown in Figure 11.1.

A very simplified version of the negotiation process is shown in Figures 11.2 and 11.3 in successful and unsuccessful versions.

In the example in Figure 11.3, the negotiating parties have started with a distributive and difficult issue: price. The negotiation is likely to get blocked or even to fail because there is not enough information at hand for the parties to resolve the problems. Wise negotiators start by building relationships and sharing information carefully as in Figure 11.2. In the end, we can come to a practical "do not" list.

- Do not be rushed.
- Do not be snowed under by data.
- Do not be too greedy.
- Do not harm others.
- Do not give something for nothing.

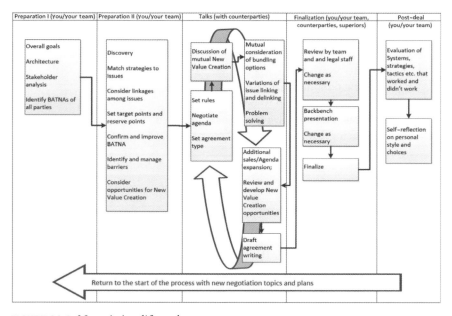

FIGURE 11.1 Negotiation life cycle

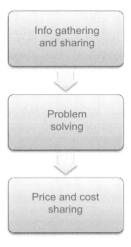

FIGURE 11.2 Successful flow – leads to completion

FIGURE 11.3 Unsuccessful flow – distributive issues blocked without information sharing

- Do not fail to learn.
- Do not fail to prepare.

Do not be rushed

Push deadlines back with superiors, clients, partners and other negotiating parties. Allow more time rather than less time in order to solve problems and create relationships that will survive fruitfully.

Do not be snowed under by data

Do not allow large amounts of data to confuse you. Data is not useful until categorized and analyzed. Use careful decision making processes and appropriate business analysis. Learn to categorize information so that you are not distracted by too much data.

Do not be too greedy

Learn to capture a reasonable amount of value so that you do not damage other parties in the negotiation. A reasonable approach will cause your reputation as a fair negotiator to develop.

Do not harm others

Never directly harm another party because your reputation will suffer. Worse, you may become a target for others trying to damage you and your business. Instead, learn to create satisfaction in all parties.

Do not give something for nothing

Giving something for nothing drains your resources. Gaining from your concessions means the gains must be of comparable value. The gains can be tangible (assets and resources) or intangible (relationship, reputation, brand, strategic position, etc.).

Do not fail to learn

Every negotiation, successful or unsuccessful, is a source of learning. Analyze the process in detail in the middle of and again shortly after completion of the negotiation.

Do not fail to prepare

There will be few successes in your career if you do not deeply know the details of the issues and the stakeholders related to it: know the people, know the facts.

Section summary

> An overall process starts with research and finishes with robust agreements. In between are many repeated steps of communicating, solving problems and deciding. Each step is an opportunity to learn, create value and find satisfaction among the participants.

APPENDIX I

Glossary

3D negotiation: involves three phases of action 1) what to do at the table; 2) designing the target agreement; and 3) setup of the overall negotiation. Lax and Sebenius (2006) wrote a book called *3D Negotiation* that has been widely translated – check to find a copy in your language.

Anchoring: setting expectations about cost and the general price range by making the first price offer. It is generally a good idea to make the first price offer based on sensible price research.

Assertive: strongly demanding.

At the table: formal negotiation time when the parties are talking. Imagine all parties sitting at a table, talking.

Away from the table: time and situations (breaks, recesses, meals, weekends, nights) when the parties are not formally negotiating.

Bargaining chip: a relatively unimportant concession that you plan to give in exchange for some concession. Sometimes these are called "sweeteners".

Bargaining/bartering: conceding low-priority items for concessions on items that are more important to you. Also called "log rolling" or making tradeoffs. This approach is practical with relatively simple issues and is often used to sweeten a proposal with concessions.

Bottom line: sometimes this phrase is used with the meaning of reserve price or point (see Reserve price or point).

BATNA: best alternative to a negotiated agreement (sometimes also called the "walk away"). BATNA is the result you would have if you did not negotiate. See Chapter 3.

Claiming value: trying to get the parts of a business arrangement that are most useful (and valuable) to you. See Chapter 1.

Concession: something that you give or receive, for example, a better price, a change of schedule or a change of product that suits the other parties.

Consensus: agreement. Negotiators manage consensus within their team, with their back table and ultimately with their counterparties.

Counterpart(y): a negotiator from the other side of the negotiating table.

Creating value: discovering new opportunities for value and profit. See Chapter 1.

Deadlock: a situation in which there is no progress and no agreement. The parties must break the deadlock or give up and follow their BATNA.

Deal: the package of issues in the negotiation. Also, the agreement.

Deal/no-deal balance: the thinking and decision making that go into agreeing or not agreeing; the considerations that lead negotiators to accept an offer or choose their BATNA.

Deal breaker/show stopper: an issue that must be resolved or it will cause the entire negotiation to fail. Obviously it is important to identify and manage these issues in advance of negotiations.

Deceit: providing information that is not true. This is almost always a bad idea. You may gain in the short term, but you may damage yourself in the long term.

Delinkage: separating an issue from other issues in the negotiation; delink if a particular issue threatens to ruin the negotiation or if you can sensibly separate groups of issues from each other.

Distributive negotiating: negotiating the sharing or claiming of limited resources (such as time, money, products, etc.) in a Win/Lose approach.

Empathy: understanding for feelings of other parties.

False concession: pretending that a concession you must give or do not care about is a concession that you did not want to give. You can trade this false concession for something of value. This strategy is not recommended – when the other side learns that they had to fight for something they could have gotten without any question, the relationship may be damaged.

FOTE: full open truthful exchange. This means telling everything to the other sides. Parties tell the whole truth, concealing nothing. This is sensible in negotiations where all sides have confidence in creating value jointly and sharing it reasonably. See POTE.

Hardball tactics: a variety of aggressive tactics such as threats, delays and so on. Basically, these are unprofessional and unsuitable for most business negotiation; however, some businesses use hardball tactics to put pressure on the other party. Having a good BATNA will protect you from most hardball tactics. At the table, hardball tactics are best met with silence or by resuming your normal questions.

Integrative negotiating: bringing together many issues in order to solve problems, maximize mutual gains, repackage and optimize and make robust agreements.

Interests: things that a negotiator (person, team, organization) wants. These things can be tangible (money, buildings, equipment, etc.) or intangible (services, pride, success, dignity, etc.)

Linkage/integration: combining and relating issues in the negotiation.

Mutual gains: solutions that benefit you and all parties in the negotiation. The benefits can be different for the different partners.

Negotiation: a discussion with the intent to agree. Discussions include the sharing of information; the making, rejecting and adjustment of offers; the solving of problems and the making of decisions and agreements. In this textbook, the topic is generally that of business, not politics, policy, hostages or other topics.

Opponent: a person or group you are fighting. Never use this word when talking about negotiating. You should never fight negotiation counterparts!

Party: a person or group in a negotiation. The same meaning as counterpart, counterparty or negotiation partner.

POTE: partial open truthful exchange. Parties tell the truth, but not the whole truth. Parties may wish to conceal certain information such as reserve price and items they want to offer as false concessions.

Principled negotiation: (sometimes called mutual gains bargaining) means trying to increase the total value of the negotiation by developing new ideas with your counterparts.

Reciprocity: (sometimes called the norm of reciprocity) refers to the back and forth sharing of information among negotiating parties. When one side gives a little, others are likely to give too. Do not give away all your information at once in order to develop a comfortable exchange of facts and ideas. Reciprocity not only relates to information – it also helps to build up the relationship.

Relationships: the long-term connection between the people and organizations in a negotiation

Reserve price or point: the maximum price a buyer is willing to pay. The minimum price a seller is willing to accept. Also called "reservation price". If the negotiation issue is not about money, reserve point means the most that a party is willing to give or accept in terms of concessions or resources. Beyond the reserve point, there is no logic in continuing the negotiation.

Stalling: intentionally wasting time to put pressure on the other side or push them into a quick, unfavorable agreement. This tactic is not recommended because time pressure is a double-edged sword!

Stereotype: a superficial description of a person based on a group, not individuals. Stereotyping leads to misunderstandings if applied to individuals. Stereotyping is only useful as a starting point for careful research into what groups and individuals expect and prefer, as well as research into their unique preferences.

Strategy: an overall approach to a negotiation. High-level strategies include compromise, collaborate, collapse and avoid. At a lower level of detail, specific strategies include the goals of the negotiation and the sequence of moves necessary to arrive at the goals.

Synergy: working together to create new benefits that parties could not manage alone.

Tactic: a specific effort to influence the negotiation, for example through behavior, framing of offers, deceit, staged release of information or increasing or decreasing the comfort level of the other parties. Tactics may be hard or soft. Soft tactics can be used to develop a negotiation. Hard tactics may bring short-term results but may also derail a negotiation.

Threats: a hardball tactic. Do not threaten your counterparts because it will damage the relationship.

Ultimatum: a strong offer or demand that must be agreed to immediately. This is a high-pressure tactic. Typically these are offered at the last moment. This tactic is easily defeated by extending your time and continuing a calm discussion.

Walking out: a hardball tactic. Only walk out if your BATNA is good enough to break off negotiations. Do not walk out in order to put pressure on the other parties.

Walk away point: the same as reserve point.

Win/Lose: a very simplified form of thinking about negotiating. Suitable only for distributive negotiations.

Win/Win: a more complex and better way of thinking about negotiating – create a deal that all sides can be satisfied with. However, an even better way is to create value for all parties by going beyond Win/Win and discovering new synergy.

You can find additional useful definitions at http://www.negotiations.com/definition and other websites.

APPENDIX II

Case simulations

Case: Inheritance far away

Theresa Powicki died at the grand old age of 97 in the city of Wellington, New Zealand. She had a reputation as an active and intelligent woman who decisively improved the quality of elementary school education in Wellington. She named her grandson Thomas as the sole beneficiary in her will* because he was the only living relative. Thomas and his lawyer are the only ones who have read the will. Thomas lives in Tokyo. He would visit his grandmother once a year during vacation or Christmas. Travel was long and expensive: ten hours of flying plus renting a car.

In the past few years, a husband and wife (Bob and Cheryl Willis), not related to Theresa, who lived in the same town often took care of the aging woman. They took her to the doctor or sometimes to church or on excursions and helped with cleaning, even inviting her to their home on holidays. The Willis family is active in the town, contributing to the homeless center and volunteering at the fire department. Bob is a junior high school teacher, and Cheryl lost her job two years ago.

After her death and after the usual taxes and legal costs, Theresa's will provided the house, its contents and about $60,000 New Zealand dollars (NZD) in cash and securities and, surprise, $500,000 NZD in gold! Apparently Theresa had wisely bought gold from Willis Metals (owned by a cousin of Bob's) in the years before it became expensive. There are many household items of value, totaling $40,000 NZD, that are part of Thomas' childhood memories. Of course, the value of these items could be great if sold carefully in the proper place and time, but they would be worth less than half that if sold suddenly at one time. The house itself is worth $220,000 NZD to $280,000 NZD, and perhaps even more if the economy improves in the next few years.

Thomas was pleasantly surprised – he had not expected so much at all. But then the will was contested by the Willises. They felt that the care they provided was worth $280,000 NZD. Thomas responded angrily, "You were just interested in getting her money, you didn't really care about her!" However, they said, "In fact, we did a lot while you did nothing. You hardly ever visited and could never help when she really needed someone. Anyway, who could have guessed she had a lot of gold?" This conversation was reported in the local newspaper.

The Willises brought the case to legal court in the city of Wellington. The judge froze the various properties until a decision could be made. Thomas had this decision to make: avoid court by taking only the remaining money and property and let the Willises have their cash, or fight the battle in court. Of course, a court battle would mean perhaps a few years of traveling back to New Zealand and lots of worries. A win for Thomas would mean a share of the inheritance being lost in fees to lawyers as well as travel. Worse, losing the fight would mean paying those expenses as well as giving up $280,000 NZD in cash.

Decision: Thomas will try negotiation to avoid going to court and to avoid paying all of the $280,000 and to avoid the expenses of travel, lawyers and so on.

*A will is a document that indicates what to do with a person's money and property after he or she dies.

1. Is this negotiation mostly distributive or mostly integrative?
2. What are the interests of Thomas?
3. What are the interests of Bob and Cheryl?
4. Are there issues other than money that Thomas could integrate into the negotiation?
5. Should Thomas, Bob and Cheryl negotiate directly or include another person(s)? if so, whom?
6. Approximately, what are the reserve points that Thomas and Bob and Cheryl should set before they start talking?
7. Is it possible for the parties to create value together?
8. What is Thomas's BATNA?
9. What is the BATNA of Bob and Cheryl?

Case: Three-way joint venture

Background

Three companies are engaging in negotiations to form a joint venture to produce an electronics product. The three companies have not done business together before, but they all have international experience. The companies include:

TouchPad, KK: A maker of electronic touch pads in Itami, Hyogo, Japan. They are seeking a contract manufacturing company to produce a new touch pad for service industry use.

Wushi Dalian: An electronics assembly company in Dalian (大连), China.
Taakto OY: A software company in Oulu, Finland.

The three companies have generally discussed their plans by email and phone, but this is the first meeting of all three. The goal of this meeting is to agree to a three-way joint venture, sharing investment, profits and risk. Roughly, the three companies, Touchpad, Wushi and Taakto, expect to have a 4:4:2 shareholding ratio, respectively.

In order to be successful, the three companies must combine their resources to collect about $12 million in contributions (cash or other). Therefore, they must consider the value of non-cash contributions such as intellectual property, facilities, skills and so on. These non-cash contributions might help to balance the cash contributions, or they might make it impossible to manage the deal. If the potential deal is not acceptable to the business needs and realities of one of the companies, then that party should decide not join the deal.

Building on the Memorandum of Understanding (MOU, see the following section), the parties must now decide how to evaluate the non-cash contributions of each. Each side can be flexible in the short term, but the long-term outcome has to be one that all parties believe is durable. Generally, the three companies expect to provide the following elements to the JV.

MOU: Taakto, Wushi, TouchPad

Each company has already agreed to a non-binding Memorandum of Understanding (MOU). The MOU includes the following text:

> The parties, TouchPad, Wushi and Taakto, announce their intent to form a joint venture (JV) with approximate shareholding of 40:40:20, respectively. The activity and field of the JV shall be *touch screen control pads* generally, with details of the following issues to be decided on during negotiations:
>
> • TouchPad intends to take the role of OEM, designing the equipment, developing the operating system, managing the overall concept and undertaking marketing, distribution, after-sales support and all interaction with customers and end users.

TABLE A2.1 TouchPad, Wushi, Taakto

TouchPad	Wushi	Taakto
Design, operating system, marketing, concept, most of the cash investment	Most of the manufacturing and all of the assembly, most of the non-cash investment	User interface, certain client and server software, post-sale monitoring, some investment in cash, some in-kind expertise

- Wushi intends to take the role of assembler with staff and facilities to assemble components, sub assemblies, housings and so on. Likewise, Wushi will directly manage certain sub-assembly and component companies that are located in China.
- Taakto intends to design and develop the user interface, certain client and server software, post–sale monitoring and some support services.

Case: OVD hosts a foreign investor and local business

General background for OVD, GlobalDesign and LCM

GlobalDesign is a Canadian company that designs and sells consumer products for daily use, including many innovative products that might be popular for a year or two or react to new technology. GD is proud that it was the first company to bring products such as protective pads and ergonomic grips to consumer electronics like tablets, smart phones and the newest wearable technology.

Previously a vertically integrated manufacturer, the company restructured in 2001 to become a designer and B2B/B2G marketing company, leaving manufacturing and retailing behind. Most of GD's manufacturing has been done in China up to now, however a series of unfortunate incidents regarding corrupt officials has made them consider doing business in Ruritania, a large and growing South East Asian country. Ruritania also does not have a snow-white reputation, but business acquaintances have said it is "not too bad". GD has reviewed several companies in Ruritania and asked Overseas Development (OVD) to arrange several meetings. The first is with LCM, a local contract manufacturing company.

OVD is a government agency. It exists to bring together foreign and local companies. OVD's charter allows it to make small investments, take an equity share up to 20 percent in new companies (JVs or independent firms) and provide expertise and facilitation in exchange for payment, a fee or an equity position. OVD is hosting the meeting in their downtown office.

LCM is a three-year-old company with a small plastics facility outside the capital city. It has successfully completed several contracts for US and Japanese firms. They are excited to meet with a large foreign company like GD.

Case: AP and Shepard Fairey and HOPE

A case of copyright infringement

In 2008, the US presidential election saw hopes and excitement arise around one candidate in particular, Barack Obama, who would later be elected. The excitement inspired numerous artists to create works based on then-candidate Obama. One of the most well-known and enduring works was created by Shepard Fairey, an artist using stencil art that had gained wide recognition. For more information about the artist, see <www.shepardfaireyprints.com> and other sources.

The artist based his work (see Figure A2.1, right) on a photograph (see Figure A2.1, left) taken by photographer Mannie Garcia, who was temporarily working for the news agency Associated Press (AP).

AP discovered the original photo was from AP in early 2010. AP was upset to discover that an image that they had ordered and paid for was being used to such wide acclaim – all of which went to Mr. Fairey. Additionally, the image came to be sold on many day-to-day objects as it became increasingly popular. The profits from these objects went to the artist, not the photographer and not AP.

AP considered legal action. However, things were not so clear. Their lawyers told them, "The picture has been changed – it will be up to a court to decide if the changes are substantial enough that it can no longer be considered the same picture. There are few guidelines and precedents for this matter, so much will be up to the judge." Further, they explained, "The ownership of the photo is also not so clear. Mr. Garcia was not a full time employee, so his images do not automatically belong to AP. At the time, he was not even a part-time worker for AP – he was a temporary hire and had not signed a contract. Even though he was paid for his time and he submitted the photos to AP, it is not completely clear who the rights for the picture belong to."

Meanwhile, the artist refused to discuss sharing the ownership of the changed image or profits from it. Fairey claimed that under the established rules and laws of "fair use", he was legally safe in his use and "reinterpretation" of the image.

With time, AP collected enough legal arguments to consider action. At the same time, Shepard Fairey considered his legal strengths and weaknesses; likewise, Garcia decided to let AP represent him. Both sides gave long thought to the potential costs of a protracted legal battle … and they decided to negotiate. But what should they agree to?

Here are some facts and estimates regarding the case:

- A court case of this sort could take six months to five years. One or both sides could maximize delays in order to drive up the costs and irritation for the other side. A single quick court action might cost $50,000. A single lengthy court battle might cost $2.5 million.
- Shepard Fairey has used the art of other artists in much of his work, ranging from his "Andre the Giant" series to commissioned work for corporate clients. A legal loss to AP would put him at risk of other lawsuits and potential losses.

- Shepard Fairey claims that he and his design company (Studio Number One) are nearly broke. This claim seems unlikely, but AP has to admit that there would be additional time and cost after winning a court case in order to get any money at all from the artist.
- AP estimates gross sales from products with the image before 2011 to be $5 million, and an additional $2 million per annum.
- Fairey currently estimates gross sales from products with the image to be $500,000, and an additional $200,000 per annum.
- Independent observers estimate gross sales from products with the image to be "closer to AP's guess".
- Fairey claims that income from the Obama poster during the election years was spent entirely on more posters – he considers this to be legally a campaign contribution.
- The cost of an independent audit would be about $50,000.
- Independent observers estimate that the total market for products with these images could range from $1 million per annum to $5 million per annum depending on the popularity of President Obama.
- AP has agreed with the photographer, Mannie Garcia, that they will represent him in the negotiations, providing some share of the agreed outcomes to him.

FIGURE A2.1 Photo and poster

The AP photo, left and the Shepard Fairey poster, right.
Source: Mannie Garcia/Shepard Fairey/AP

Your assignment

Represent your client (AP/Garcia or Shepard Fairey) and come to an agreement about at least the following points:

- sharing of profits up to the time of agreement;
- sharing of profits after this agreement;
- statements by either side to the public in general;
- protecting AP photos;
- other issues, if any.

Determine your goals, your reserve positions for your goals, your BATNA and who will participate in the actual negotiation at the table.

Case: Shoe business coopetition

General information

Mr. Tang and Mr. Lee were colleagues in a division of the company Runaway Sports[1] in 1993, devoting their personal time to developing a unique, dual-purpose roller-skate sneaker. For over three years, Tang and Lee devoted their evenings and weekends to the project, working through the research and development (R&D) process. The various expenses of developing drawings and a 3D prototype were financed by Tang Industries[2] – Mr. Tang's father's family business. The unique roller-skate sneaker was thus developed in Taiwan, and a patent was first granted in Taipei in 1999 and classified as an invention[3] type of patent. Tang and Lee shared time developing their ideas, investing in the product as a joint business venture to generate lucrative profits. Further patent applications regarding this roller-skate sneaker were submitted to over 50 countries in East Asia, Central and Western Europe and North America. At this point, Tang and Lee left their day jobs to work full-time developing their own business.

The original prototype was considered the personal property of both Tang and Lee – under patent law, each co-inventor named on the patent application owns that property. Patent law gives co-owners of a patent the right to make, use, license, sell and import the patented invention. Having gained the official patent license, Tang and Lee shared the rights to their exclusive product. The priority of the patent right prohibits other parties from producing imitation goods in the countries where the patent has been granted, acting as protection against intellectual infringement. Upon release, both Tang and Lee had legal claim to future revenue, and for a while both Tang and Lee seemed content.

History between Tang and Lee

Of the two, Tang was the more business savvy. Tang had an eye for detail and benefited from having a strong family network, as Tang's father was a well-respected entrepreneur with manufacturing plants throughout Southeast Asia. Lee's physics background helped distinguish what they were offering. His technical knowledge was fundamental to the product's inventiveness. Lee was confident that the design and appearance of the prototype was sure to be a smash hit, and his production design was both sleek and functional. The prototype was to be the first dual-purpose shoe of its kind, and although the R&D costs were substantial, both men were confident that they could recoup the costs relatively quickly. Up until this point, Tang's family had financed the project from conception through R&D and also through initial production, as Tang and Lee had encountered problems getting credit to manufacture at the scale they desired.

Between 1999 and early 2001, patent applications in over 50 countries were granted, and the prototype was launched and distributed throughout the world. The shoe sold especially well in the domestic market of Taiwan, as what they had developed was truly original. The annual revenue of this sneaker from global sales and patent authorizations to other firms was $100,000 USD. Tang valued Lee's sense of design and agreed to share future profits with him on a 50–50 basis, despite Tang's family having financed the R&D costs, estimated at $40,000 USD. Their sneakers were marketed towards kids and teenagers.

Conflicting interests

Lee thought Tang was taking credit for his contribution, and the two had conflicting ideas on how the original prototype might be improved. Unexpectedly and rather quickly, Tang and Lee parted company in late 2001, soon after the original prototype patent had been granted. Lee left Tang and moved to Europe to establish his own company within two years. Tang also established his own business in 2001 as a sub-unit of his father's business enterprise and utilized his family's network connections to distribute the roller-skate sneaker, as his father's business had trade links throughout Asia and the Far East.

From 2001 to 2003, both entrepreneurs implemented individual business strategies and important new products loosely based upon the original roller-skate sneaker. In 2013, Tang and Lee both released their own second-generation roller-skate sneakers based on their initial prototype. Tang released his second-generation sneaker in November 2013 and mainly applied for patent design and patent utility. Lee realized his second-generation sneaker in March 2013 with a pending patent in invention and utility. Their second-generation patents had unique attributes, and the shoes themselves were redesigned for customers with different needs. The key features of Tang's second-generation shoe included a cool and easy adhesive strapping. The shoes were hard-wearing and featured a cushioned sole. Lee's second-generation sneaker included a shock-absorbing, foam-based material located in the shoe's sole, inspired by his background in physics. Bitter rivals, Tang and Lee quarreled over who had had the original idea and spent a small fortune securing patents in a variety of domains but also on litigation, suing one another over breach of intellectual property and ownership.

Marketing positioning

In keeping with Tang's price point, Tang's roller-skate sneaker became especially popular in the Far East as his shoe was substantially cheaper (40 percent) to manufacture than the competition in Europe. Lee's roller-skate sneaker was more stylish, comfortable and sold well to fashion conscious Europeans. His business had to absorb higher production costs and focused on developing products that were truly innovative.

The two sports shoe entrepreneurs became bitter rivals, doing whatever they could to get an edge over the other. Neither Tang nor Lee were beyond

TABLE A2.2 Tang and Lee second-generation products

Second generation	Manufacturing price/pair	Manufacturing location	Market price/pair	Product key characteristic
Tang's shoe	$5–$7 USD	South Asia	$13–$17 USD	Fair value
Lee's shoe	$8.5–$11.5 USD	Europe	$18–$26 USD	Fashion

TABLE A2.3 Tang and Lee comparison

Background	Employees	Firm's turnover	Granted patents since 2001	Key business network
Tang's firm	12 people	$850,000 USD	1 invention 3 utilities 5 designs	South American countries and East and Middle Asian merging countries
Lee's firm	5 people	$450,000 USD	4 inventions 4 utilities 15 designs	European and North American countries

poaching staff, and occasionally would go out of their way to put the other's product in a less than positive light.

It took many years before Tang and Lee could discuss matters rationally. Not wanting to meet face-to-face, they appointed their trusted business advisors to seek out an amicable solution to resolve their long-standing dispute. As Mr. Lee' trusted business advisor, Helmut is expected to find a satisfactory solution to please his client. Wei Wei is a trusted business advisor of Mr. Tang, and she is expected to find a beneficial solution for her client. Both Helmut and Wei Wei are patent clerks in private commercial firms, and have arranged to discuss their clients' concerns and negotiate on behalf of Tang and Lee to find a mutually beneficial and satisfactory solution.

Note: A patent clerk in commercial enterprise is often an investigator charged with examining patent applications to provide consulting opinions to patent applicants regarding whether a claimed invention could be potentially awarded a patent. Generally speaking, the most important task of a patent clerk is to review the technical information disclosed in a patent application. This involves reading and understanding a particular application and then searching to determine what technological contribution the application provides to the public.

A patent is awarded for informing the public about special technical details of a new invention, so the work of a patent clerk involves searching existing patents, scientific journals, data resources and other material for prior artwork (diagrams, etc.) and to verify an application to determine whether it complies with the legal requirements. These requirements are often substantially different depending on the country in which the patent has been registered.

Further questions for consideration

- What are the distinguishing attributes of their positions?
- What are the dispute points?
- What do Tang and Lee stand to gain by pooling their resources?

[1] a fabricated company name
[2] a fabricated company name
[3] There are three categories of patent in Taiwan: invention, utility and design.

- Invention: a creation from a technical concept based on the laws of nature (20 years duration).
- Utility: a creation that has been made in respect of the form, construction or fitting of an object (ten years duration).
- Design: a creation made in respect to the shape, pattern, color or their combination of an article (12 years duration).

Case: ZawaSoft and Pak-Ton

Background information

ZawaSoft and Pak-Ton are considering a partnership. ZawaSoft's new "On the Spot" software makes it possible for Pak-Ton's electronic batteries to last three times longer. Pak-Ton would like to license the technology from ZawaSoft for its products (electronic batteries for small electronic equipment up to 1kg). ZawaSoft has three shareholders, each with a 20 percent share. According to newspaper reports, the shareholders are aggressive about seeking profits within a one to two year timescale.

Pak-Ton was established by a committed Zen Buddhist – this philosophy and system of ethics remains a basis of the company today. Pak-Ton publishes a quarterly newsletter relating their business and ethics to Buddhism and has annual events with temples near company offices and plants.

Case: Recruit the best!

Recruit the best!

FC Nürnburg is a club in the top league of Germany, the Bundesliga. The club competes against top teams like Munich, Hamburg and so on. Although Nürnburg has always been in this league, it has never won the title and seldom performs strongly. The past two years, however, have seen a significant improvement in the quality of play and players and the number of victories. The club's fortunes appear to be headed upward!

This year FC Nürnburg is recruiting another leading player onto the team. Financial resources are limited of course, so they are aiming to get only one player. They hope they have found their new star in the person of Bolas Chojonez. Chojonez is a shy and religious person who taught swimming safety in his home country (which he misses) and famously rescued two children from a flood there. He swims daily.

Chojonez arrived from his native home of Philippines to the league below Nürnburg's two years ago. Each year he has improved, especially last year. His opportunity to leap into one of Europe's leading leagues has come! It is this league that has produced World Cup winners and legendary individuals, teams and coaches for 40 years.

Chojonez is now 19 years old, considered young for a football player. If he can avoid injuries, he may have ten to 12 years of good football ahead of him. Chojonez is considered among the top players of the lower league, but has not been ranked within the Bundesliga.

The Nürnburg team pays starting squad players an average of €500,000 per season (there are 18 games in a season), usually minus 5 percent for every missed game (if the game is missed due to injuries, the player loses only 2 percent). First-year members are usually paid less. In addition to the 11 starting team members, there are 20 other members who play on practice teams and occasionally join the main team. These players earn an average of €150,000 annually.

FC Nürnburg has a strong connection to the city's community. Players appear in public at kids' programs and other events frequently throughout the year. Popular players attract many daily emails and letters as well as fans with signs at games; therefore, shirts with their name and number sell well.

Your task

Please come to an agreement that covers at least the following contract issues:

- salary;
- number of years;
- illness/injury compensation.
    It is of course acceptable to come to no agreement.

Case: Sonde SA strikes a balance

General information for all participants

The Japanese affiliate (in Osaka) of Sonde SA has a small number of French expatriates on the sales and design team – only ten. Of these, five change annually, meaning that each person is in Japan for two years. These expatriates arrive and leave with the Japanese fiscal year (April–March). They expect to take three to four weeks of vacation in August like most people in France; however, they are instead limited to a few days during *Obon*, a three-day national vacation. As a result, several of them stay home "sick" for a week or more in August and/or September. At the end of two years, they generally stop working early in March, staying home for almost one month. They say they are sick, but probably they go bicycling in the countryside!

This intercultural simulation includes five roles. There are two French roles (the site CEO and a representative of the French workers) and three Japanese roles (human resources manager, the head of the sales and design team and a low level supervisor).

The French staff complains about the short vacation time loudly and long each year.

Your job is to find a suitable solution. You will discuss and interact with the following people:

- HRM chief manager;
- head of sales and design team;
- French CEO of Japanese affiliate;
- Japanese supervisor of the design team;
- French worker (sales and design team member).

See Appendix VII for materials for each of the previous five roles.

Case: Cultural IP anime

Background

PXWX of Hangzhou, China is an animation firm that provides animation services to various Japanese animation studios. The studios in Japan develop the main content, ideas, characters, style and stories. PXWX usually provides services such as coloring, background and the many drawings that fill in the movement between key pictures. This relationship has been stable for about ten years, during which time PXWX has steadily increased its gross revenues, number of contracts and number of customers in Japan.

RekiMan of Hirakata, Japan became a customer of PXWX about four years ago and has enjoyed a good relationship with PXWX during that time. RekiMan specializes in animations of historical material and folktales targeting young adults.

Last year, PXWX began its first original animation series. It is for the Chinese market. PXWX developed the style, characters, stories, all animation sequences...everything, releasing the first series of ten episodes to wide domestic acclaim. In the development process, the storyboards (a series of pictures outlining the action) of an episode were accidentally sent to RekiMan. RekiMan quickly returned the materials to PXWX with encouraging comments about the quality of the materials and PXWX's project in general.

PXWX, however, only last week, was horrified to find that a work order from RekiMan included a set of storyboards strikingly similar to the ones PXWX had accidently sent to RekiMan. PXWX was incensed!

They immediately notified RekiMan that they would start legal action for theft of intellectual property in the Hangzhou city court system. PXWX was quoted in a news article in the *Hangzhou Business Press* complaining about RekiMan's piracy. Further, they told RekiMan that work would immediately stop on the current project, though the contract was 20 percent ($300,000) prepaid and only 10 percent of the work has been done. Finally, they told RekiMan to stop work on their Yamashiro White Snake project in Japan or face additional legal action in Japan.

RekiMan responded that they had in no way stolen anything from PXWX and proposed negotiations to avoid court proceedings that would destroy the relationship and be pointlessly expensive. PXWX, feeling somewhat less heated, agreed to listen.

Case: Toyota Tsusho and Encana – second round

Background for Toyota Tsusho and Encana

In April 2012, Toyota Tsusho and Encana announced an agreement in which Toyota Tsusho would pay $602 million to gain 32.5 percent of Encana's Horseshoe Canyon field. This field produces so-called dry gas from coal beds at relatively shallow depths.

The development of coal bed methane (CBM) gas is not too expensive because wells are neither deep nor high pressure. However, when a field is mature, it does not produce gas so quickly. How much gas remains in a developed dry gas field like the Horseshoe Canyon play is quite well understood, so it is usually possible to know when the field will be depleted and when the remaining gas will require special expensive efforts to recover.

The 2012 deal includes 4000 existing wells and 1500 future wells. The field has been in production for many years and the geology (and output) is very well understood and very predictable. The deal is a royalty interest deal in which Toyota Tsusho will get 32.5 percent of the gas produced.

Toyota Tsusho was quite satisfied with the 2012 deal: it captured a long-term supply of easy-to-handle gas with easily predictable maintenance and running costs. So Toyota Tsusho sent its accountants to sharpen their pencils and found some additional money it could use for more gas field investment.

Toyota Tsusho and Encana are preparing new negotiations for other gas fields or additional investment in some of the remaining part of Encana's Horseshoe Canyon play that is not part of the original agreement (now part of Prairie Sky Royalty). Encana holds 60 percent (78 million shares) of this company.

With Japan's nuclear power plants almost all closed and unlikely to restart soon and access to oil from Iran, Russia and other countries seemingly always at risk, the appeal of energy from a politically reliable source is great. Canada, a politically stable energy exporter, is a great potential partner. Moreover, gas is much cleaner than the coal that Japan imports from Australia, China, Indonesia and North America. Japan consumes about 4,500 billion cubic feet of natural gas annually, and about 4,300 billion cubic feet are imported. Total [annual] primary energy consumption in Japan is over 20 quadrillion British thermal units (Btu) (US Energy Information Agency, 2013).

In recent years, North American gas-producing companies are avoiding investment in CBM as the price of gas has declined since 2011 and recovered only recently to prices between $3.50 and $4.00 per million BTU. Price forecasts are unclear. Even though most power plants in North America have switched to gas from coal, supply seems likely to stay ahead of demand.

In 2012, ConocoPhillips announced, "ConocoPhillips will virtually cease capital spending on North American dry natural gas assets to focus on projects that offer higher returns" (Magill, 2012). For that company, and others, it meant a focus on oil and wet gas. The term "wet gas" refers to natural gas that includes many complex hydrocarbons, including highly valuable liquids (condensates). These liquids are easy to transport (no condensing equipment or pressurized pipeline needed), require less processing than crude oil and command a high price. Dry gas, on the other hand, has less value and is usually transported continuously and efficiently by pipeline, but requires very little processing.

Encana has developed the Horseshoe Canyon play in accordance with the Toyota Tsusho agreement, drilling in 2013 approximately 238 net natural gas wells and 45 net oil wells. Production after royalties averaged approximately 335 MMcf/d of natural gas and approximately 9.9 Mbbls/d of oil and NGLs. As of 31 December 2013, this play included approximately 1.7 million gross undeveloped acres (1.5 million net acres) that Encana controlled (EDGAR SEC, 2014, p. 11). For the purpose of this negotiation, the 1.7 million acres previously mentioned are not available for discussion.

Gas prices appear to be recovering in North America, however most analysts predict long-term oversupply. The light line in the graph in Figure A2.2 shows the change in natural gas prices in North America from Summer 2013 to Summer 2014. The dark line shows the change in oil prices over the same time. Wise negotiators will update the following information at any of several websites with commodities data.

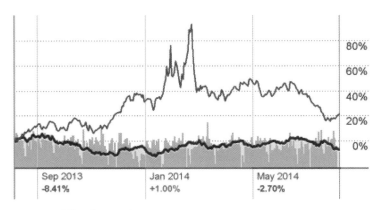

FIGURE A2.2 Oil and gas price movements

Source: money.cnn.com

Useful jargon for all parties

- Bbl: a unit measure of oil, one barrel of oil. One bbl = 158.98 liters.
- Btu: British thermal unit. A measure of energy, one cubic foot of natural gas contains about 1030 Btu. Japan uses about 20,000,000,000,000,000 Btu of energy (all sources) annually.
- CBM: Coal bed methane, gas that comes from coal located in the ground.
- Condensate: natural gas condensate. A range of chemicals found in natural gas and oil that can be used for making fuel or plastics. These must be separated from the widely used dry natural gas that is transported in pipelines and tanks to point of use. The separation of condensates from gas usually occurs at the wellhead or a processing facility in the pipeline. Condensates are inexpensive to refine further (oil, for example, is more expensive and complex to refine).

Condensate types (C1 – C5)

C1: methane (dry gas). The "liquid rich" gases are:
C2: Ethane
C3: Propane
C4: Butane
C5: Condensate (liquid, not a gas, composed of various hydrocarbon chemicals)

- Dry gas: gas that comes out of the ground with few or no condensates. Generally, gas from coal beds (CBM) is dry.

- Flaring: the practice of burning unused gas at the wellhead. This practice is targeted by environmentalists as destructive and wasteful.
- Play: the meaning of "a play" in the oil and gas industry is an opportunity to get resources from a certain geology. Example: Barnett shale oil in Texas is a play that refers to oil in a certain kind of rock found at a certain depth in a certain region. The Alberta Bakken play means oil and gas in a layer of rock covering more than 500,000 km² below the surface in Saskatchewan, Manitoba, North Dakota and Western Montana. Many other wet and dry gas plays exist in North America.
- Royalty interest: "In the oil and gas industry this refers to ownership of a portion of the resource or revenue that is produced. A company or person that owns a royalty interest does not bear any of the costs of the operations needed to produce the resource, yet the person or company still owns a portion of resource of revenue produced" (Investopedia, 2015).
- Shallow gas wells: like CBM wells, these are usually low pressure and therefore relatively cheap to build and maintain.
- Wellhead: the point where the gas or oil well breaks the surface. The wellhead is a structure immediately below and above ground that safely maintains pressure and strength. If a wellhead fails, there is usually an explosion, fire and tremendous damage.
- Wet gas: two meanings: 1) natural gas that comes out of the well with high levels of condensates, or 2) gas that occurs with water coming out of the well. The water must be disposed of (expensive and requires special plans and permits).

Cubic feet

Mcf: thousands of cubic feet
MMcf: millions of cubic feet
Bcf: billions of cubic feet
Tcf: trillions of cubic feet
One cubic foot = 0.0283 cubic meter
One cubic foot = 28.3 liters

Case: Channel-Port aux Basques

General Information Port-aux-Basques and AFD

Channel-Port aux Basques is a town of old fishing villages. It is one of the oldest continually inhabited towns in Newfoundland, Canada, founded in

FIGURE A2.3 Newfoundland, Canada

Source: Google Maps

the 1680s by Basque fishermen from France and Spain. Prior to that, Basque, French, Portuguese and Spanish fishermen visited irregularly to trade with the aboriginal population, starting in the mid-1500s. The town is some 900 km east of the city of St John's, Newfoundland's main city. The economy is supported mainly by the Marine Atlantic ferry terminal, which connects the Newfoundland to Nova Scotia. In addition to the maritime history, the remains of the rail station and some old boats make the town an interesting historical location. The city managers will meet with a development agency to seek funding to improve the local economy.

Case: Three party email negotiation – residential real estate

General information for all parties

The following case is to be conducted by email only. The three parties are:

- vender – seller of the property, Mrs. Lee;
- real estate agent – Wang Homes;
- buyer – Mr. and Mrs. Pim (Thai couple).

The housing market in Asia has been growing. Lately, Asia-Pacific housing markets are getting stronger (for more information see Global Property Guide, 2014b). There are more and more foreign and overseas buyers who are finding property prices affordable in Malaysia. People now want to sell their homes, as they stand a better chance of getting a good price for their property. Properties are selling very quickly. The difficulty of finding reasonable prices is causing the housing market to inflate. From a buyer's perspective, a new influx of homes has come to market, giving buyers more opportunities to invest in different types of properties. Real estate agents are pleased to see new opportunities opening up.

A married couple, Mr. and Mrs. Pim, are planning on settling down and are considering raising a family together. After discussing mortgage advice with various bankers, they are aware of how much they are able to borrow. They have a good credit history and have incurred no debts of any kind. Mr. and Mrs. Pim hold bank accounts in both Singapore and Malaysia, and bank with the same globally recognized financial institution.

Currently, Mr. and Mrs. Pim rent temporary accommodations in a suburb of Kuala Lumpur (for more information see Global Property Guide, 2014a), Malaysia, near to Mrs. Pim workplace, and a second apartment in a quiet and safe area, close by Mr. Pim's retired parents in Singapore. Despite living in Malaysia for over three years, neither Mr. Pim nor Mrs. Pim speaks fluent Malay or English. Mr. Pim speaks no Malay whatsoever and spends at least six months of the year in Singapore, working in the music industry. Due to the disadvantage of language, the couple would like to use email to communicate and negotiate with the real estate agency in Malaysia.

Mr. and Mrs. Pim have been actively searching for a house in March and would like to have their own home by summertime. Mrs. Lee is a teacher and would like to sell her house before the new term starts. The real estate agency Wang Homes is responsible to Mrs. Lee for selling her house in Kuala Lumpur, Malaysia (see the house brochure, Ref. KLA03A, that follows).

How to conduct this negotiation

This is a five-day email negotiation. Participants are encouraged to plan their e-negotiation strategy in advance. There is a suggested maximum of ten emails that may be exchanged between each party. The rules are simple:

- a maximum of ten individual e-mails may be exchanged between the buyer and the agent;
- a maximum of ten individual e-mails may be exchanged between the vender and the agent;
- there is no word limitation and attachments are also permitted.

TABLE A2.4 Three party email negotiation: issues and initial planning

Cost	Buyer	Seller	Agent
Renovation	9,000 MYR	20,000 MYR (18 months)	No sale, no fee. The higher the agent's fee, the lower the solicitor's fee.
White goods	Not in the budget	3,000 MYR (six months)	

(Continued)

TABLE A2.4 (Continued)

Cost	Buyer	Seller	Agent
New furniture	Not in the budget	7,000 MYR (18 months)	
House movers	1000 MYR	1,000 MYR (furniture)	
House gain tax		30 percent of gain above 220,000 5000 MYR or 10 percent exemption	
Agent's fee	Included in house sale		
Solicitor's fee	0.75 percent of the cost of the house sale that excludes the agent's fee		
Stamp duty	100,000 for 1 percent above to 275,000 for 2 percent		
Others	900 MYR (rental)		
Example	If the house is sold for 275,000 MYR inclusive of 2.75 percent agent's fee (7562): • The solicitor's fee: $(275,000 - 7562) \times 0.007 = 1872$ • The stamp duty fee: $100,000 \times 0.01 + 175,000 \times 0.02 = 4,500$ • The total cost of the house, including legal fees, is 281,372 MYR.		
BATNA	Other house 299,000 MYR or Property in Singapore (more expensive, and more likely to be an apartment).	Share the cost of the agent's fee between buyer and seller. Play time and await a higher offer, but risk sacrificing the down payment on new property.	Reducing agent's fee for the seller. Suggesting both parties split the agent fee.
RP	275,000 MYR of house sale price	Furniture inclusive	
Asking price	256,000 MYR	275,000 MYR	
Walk away	300,000 MYR, including all costs	250,000 MYR (about to lose profit)	

TABLE A2.5 Three party email negotiation: value claiming by party

Party	Motive	Needs	Value-claiming points
The buyer	Raising a family	Close to transportation links No vehicle Have little money Time pressure on housing market Avoid addition rent in Kuala Lumpur	First time buyer No house chain Quick transaction Bank's initial agreement No sale, agent makes no bonus
The agency	Getting bonus (source of majority of income)	Linking the interests of both parties	Strategic advantages of the location Fairly new renovation condition. Good transportation links Ready to move in condition Quick sale to reduce time pressure Company resources Before the new term starts A minimum value is set at 250,000 MYR for foreign buyer
The seller	Moving with Mr. Lee	Down payment Time urgency on down payment	Found the property Ready to move out Selling pieces of furniture or white goods Good taste on the house Highlighting the second house project with the same estate agent No sale, agent has no bonus

For the seller, deciding how to sell

If you can't sell your home to the buyer, you may wish to take into account whether the buyer:

- is a first-time buyer;
- has found a buyer for their own property. If so, is it part of the chain of buying and selling and how long is the chain;

- is your buyer paying cash, or are they more likely to get a mortgage;
- wants to move at the same time as you.

Five notes on selling

1) Price – a person can generally sell a house by lowering the price.
2) Differentiation from the neighbors – make the house memorable (e.g. note high-grade windows, new roof, custom designs and improvements such as a patio or conservatory).
3) Appearances count – remove all clutter from inside and outside of the building. Potential buyers want to see a clean and tidy house that is spacious.
4) Sweeten the pot – another way to attract buyers is to offer incentives. For example, offer to reduce fees for a quick sale or offer to pay the cost of moving. Offer a transferable warranty or offer to introduce them to what is available in the neighborhood.
5) Improve curb appeal – remove unsightly shrubbery. Paint the front door or patch-up the drive. The first thing a buyer sees is a house's external appearance, and the way it looks compared with the surrounding neighborhood will set your property apart.

For the buyer, how much do you want for your home

The estate agent in Singapore or Malaysia is responsible for obtaining potential buyers. The agent would try to get the best possible price for the seller. Just remember, the seller does not have to accept the first offer put to them. The seller shouldn't be rushed into making a decision he/she may regret.

Decide what you are looking for in a property – whether you require parking and/or a garden, a specific number of bedrooms, the style and period may also be relevant, etc. Most importantly, consider what you want out of the location – schools, commuting convenience, shopping, noise levels and so on – do your research. This is likely to be your biggest personal financial outlay in your life, so visit several properties and be selective.

Accepting an offer

Even if the seller has accepted an offer, there is nothing unlawful about a change of mind and accepting a higher offer from someone else before you have exchanged the fee to take the seller's home off the market. The seller should also bear in mind that when an offer is made and accepted, the potential buyer has the option to change his/her mind. The buyer has 14 working days in which to withdraw.

Legal work

After the seller has accepted an offer, he/she is required to inform whoever is doing the legal work. In both Singapore and Malaysia, this is done by either a solicitor or licensed conveyancer. In Malaysia, a solicitor works on behalf of both parties – seller and buyer. Recently, however, it is becoming increasingly common for both parties to be represented by individual solicitors: one for the buyer and a second representing the seller.

When foreigners purchase any kind of property, the minimum value is set at 250,000 MYR (for more information see Global Property Guide, 2014a). To take the advertisement off the market, a letter of offer/acceptance must be signed, and a 3 percent deposit is expected from the buyer. Then, the sale and purchase agreement must be signed within 14 days and stamped at the Stamp Office. It suggests the buyer have a 14-day cooling off period, during which time they could abandon the project; however, they would lose the deposit. From the date of signing, the buyer has three months (maximum) to complete the full transaction.

Ref. KLA03A

Wang Homes

House in Sri Hartamas

275,000 MYR INC.

Attractive, semi-detached townhouse built in 1900, with an art-nouveau exterior. This period property is situated in the residential area of Sri Hartamas, near Ampang. The neighborhood has access to restaurants and a supermarket. The property includes four generous bedrooms, office and a large living room leading to a modern fitted kitchen. The property also includes two bathrooms. The ground floor has access to two large storage spaces. Total living space is 130m². Excellent transportation links: a 350m walk to two bus stations and 800m to a metro station. Energy performance certification is rated at the level of Standard.

Characteristics

Year	1900 established	**Garage**	No, shared driveway at rear
Type	Semi-detached house	**Kitchen**	Separate kitchen
Interior	Excellent, art–nouveau design	**Transport**	Metro and bus
Energy	Boiler (six years old)	**Windows**	Single–glazing throughout, with authentic art characteristics

Flooring	Original oak-flooring	**Garden**	No, terrace decking
House tax	800 MYR/year	**Cellar**	No, but two large storages
Community charge	No	**Bathroom**	Two bathrooms and two toilets

Ground floor

Entrance: 8.5m²
Storage underneath stair: 1m²
Tiled flooring
Toilet with basin: 2.5m²
Shared driveway (45 m²) with two further storage spaces towards the rear of the house (10/12m²)

First floor

Landing and hallway: 7m²
Living room and dining space: 42m²
Terrace: wood decking 20m²
Office: 4m²

Second floor

Landing and hallway: 4m²
Two bedrooms: 13.5m²
En suite bedroom: 16m²
Bathroom: 7.5m² (including wash basin, toilet and bathtub)

Third floor (attic)

Hallway: 2m²
Two bedrooms: 9/11m²
Note: The house price with INC, indicates that the agent fee is included in the house sale.

APPENDIX III

Planning documents

Issue/reserve planning document, Brett

TABLE A3.1 Brett planning sheet, blank

Issue	Self		Other	
	Reserve		**Reserve**	
BATNA				
Overall Goals				

Source: Brett, 2007 [CD].

Planning document – clusters

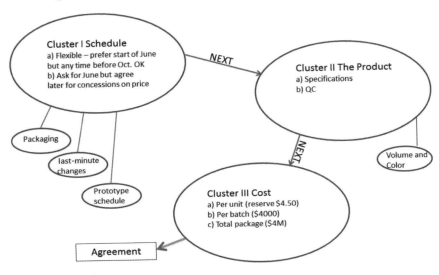

FIGURE A3.1 Cluster planning

Cluster planning is most useful for complex negotiations with multiple parties.

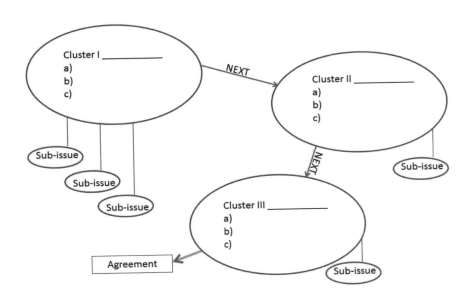

FIGURE A3.2 Cluster planning, blank

Reserve line

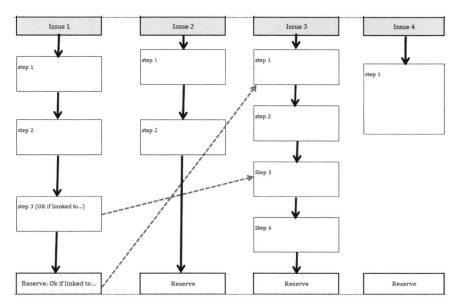

FIGURE A3.3 Reserve line planning

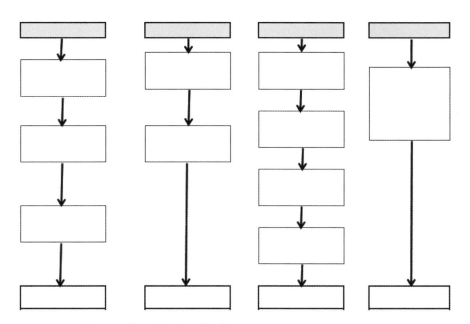

FIGURE A3.4 Reserve line planning, blank

Backward planning

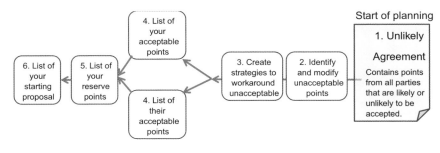

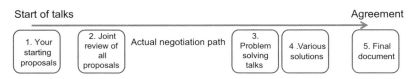

FIGURE A3.5 Backward planning

Source: Developed based on Lax and Sebenius, 2006, p. 234.

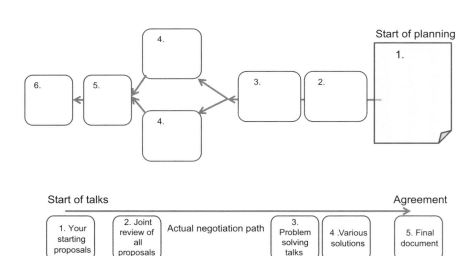

FIGURE A3.6 Backward planning, blank

Source: Developed based on Lax and Sebenius, 2006, p. 234.

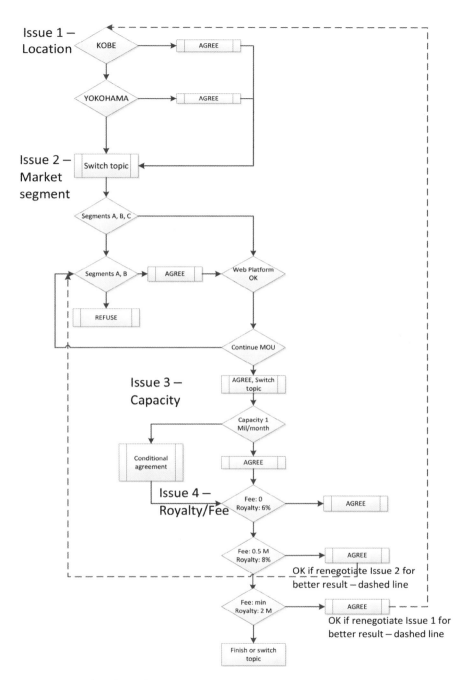

Issue 1 — Location

KOBE

AGREE

YOKOHAMA

AGREE

Issue 2 — Market segment

Switch topic

Segments A, B, C

Segments A, B

AGREE

Web Platform OK

REFUSE

Continue MOU

Issue 3 — Capacity

AGREE, Switch topic

Capacity 1 Mil/month

Conditional agreement

AGREE

Issue 4 — Royalty/Fee

Fee: 0 Royalty: 6%

AGREE

Fee: 0.5 M Royalty: 8%

AGREE

OK if renegotiate Issue 2 for better result — dashed line

Fee: min Royalty: 2 M

AGREE

OK if renegotiate Issue 1 for better result — dashed line

Finish or switch topic

FIGURE A3.7 Flowchart planning

TABLE A3.2 Modified Raiffa scorecard

Issue	Points (max)	Steps	Step points	Linked issues	Notes
Control of product	25	1. Control creation and design of all new products	25		
		2. Share creation of new products, but all must be organic	18	OK if we agree to relationship longer than 5 years	
		3. Agree that existing products will not change; no control of new products	10	OK if we get low price on investment funding and no limit on distribution	
Length of agreement	20	Agreed 5+ years exclusive cooperation	20		
		2 years exclusive cooperation	10		
		1–2 years, not exclusive	5	Must increase price	

TABLE A3.3 Modified blank Raiffa scorecard

Issue	Issue points	Steps	Step points	Linked issues	Notes

Flowchart planning

This kind of chart takes some skill and practice to design, but it is very good for your planning.

Diamonds show steps, and the last one in a series indicates the reserve. Notes explain links among issues.

Issues, steps, reserve, scorecard

This planning document (a modified Raiffa scorecard) helps you to track the positions between your preferred (1) and least desirable (reserve) steps. You can include notes about linked issues or how to handle them in the negotiation.

APPENDIX IV

Negotiation errors

Error: how not to give a concession

Extract 4 (*continued*)

5	Seller S	like er * well 2.16 million * an' because of the
6		purchasing policies an' things like this we reduced
7		the price okay we took out some things like the
8		neutral air (-) [cubicle but we
9		(CLEARS THROAT)]
10	Seller.J	didn't take out much more than 80 thousand [pounds
11	BuyerS	mm]
12	Seller.J	worth but we give you a 365 k reduction ** to bring it
13		down to this 179|5. . .
		(part of discussion has been omitted)]
14	Seller.J	we wanna be partners with you an' if we can help * so
15		we did it that's what I'm saying so this 1795 is of our
16		good will without being asked
17	SellerA	can I take another (-) to that also in that period we
18		have lost 20%
19	SellerJ	yeah I'll show you this actually
20	SellerP	yeah
21	SellerA	on the currency
. . .		(part of discussion has been omitted)
22	BuyerL	sorry] sorry that the Finnish mark is getting weaker **
23	SellerA	no the Finnish mark is [getting stronger
24	SellerP	[stronger]
25	SellerJ	stronger]. . .

Source: Used with permission, Vuorela, 2005.

Analysis questions:

What did the sales team give? _____ Why?

_____

What did the buyers give? _____ Why?

_____

What do you think happened to the sales team after this?

_____

Write a sentence or two for the sales team to correctly offer this discount:

_____

_____

_____

Negotiator's Oath, according to Simon Hazeldine in *Bare Knuckle Negotiating* (2006, p. 54):

I solemnly promise never to give something for nothing!

Error: when to go slow

TABLE A4.1 Error: when to go slow

Nonaka: Let's start with the price – is $5.50 per unit OK? Tanaka: Sure! Now let's talk about delivery time.	Nonaka should now realize that $5.50 was very favorable for Tanaka. Nonaka should have opened higher to gain value for his company.

What can Nonaka do? The opportunity to get a higher price has gone. The opportunity to get a concession for coming down has gone. Nonaka can try to be more careful on another issue and link it to the price.

Nonaka: OK, delivery time. This is difficult for us because of the busy season. We are scheduling the work for the end of October. Tanaka: We need to get the work somewhat sooner . . . Nonaka: Sooner? Do you mean September? Tanaka: Actually early August would be the best. Nonaka: We could manage that, but set up and preparation will not be as efficient. If you are willing to pay a little more, $6.25, we would be able to manage around the first week of September. Tanaka: Well, in that case . . .	Now Nonaka has made an offer and found out more about what Tanaka needs. Nonaka's offer is well structured, getting plus $0.75 but not committing to an exact time. Now, Tanaka has a reason to consider paying more and the two parties can explore the situation constructively. In the end, Nonaka can drop the price again, but only if there is a gain in some tangible or intangible way that is important.

But let's think about Tanaka's quick answer, "Sure!" What did that quick answer signal to Nonaka? By answering so quickly, Tanaka let Nonaka know that the price was too low. As a result, Nonaka knew to try to increase the price. Nonaka is a smart negotiator who got good value for his company without damaging the other company.

Error: watch your BATNA

The following case shows a major US company that could not back out of a project after a public commitment that damaged their BATNA.

Case: The very public offer

In 2011, Hewlett Packard (HP), the well-known electronics company that led Silicon Valley from its earliest days, acquired Autonomy, a leading UK software and services provider.

In early summer 2011, the CEO of HP, Leo Apotheker, and his counterpart at Autonomy, Mike Lynch, discussed the possibility of an acquisition. At the same time, other US companies considered making offers to buy Autonomy. In the following weeks, however, those other companies rejected acquiring Autonomy. Nonetheless, on 18 August, HP announced in a press release that they would attempt to take over Autonomy, paying about $10.25 billion, a 64 percent premium to the stock price. The same press release announced the closing of HP's $40 billion personal computer business and the WebOS tablet and smartphone division, in order to refocus on software services. Lastly, the press release disclosed that HP held $13 billion in cash for any and all business use.

Autonomy, meanwhile, had run out of potential buyers. With the formal acquisition offer, HP would have to pay significant penalties in the UK for cancelling the takeover, unless serious troubles came to light on the side of Autonomy.

Observers and analysts immediately criticized HP's plans and their stock priced dropped significantly, from about $32 to about $23 that week. The CEO was severely criticized and then fired on 22 September. On 28 September, Oracle released a statement that they had found Autonomy too expensive at about $6 billion (Oracle, 2011). Nonetheless, the new CEO at HP, Meg Whitman, approved the acquisition at a premium greater than 70 percent on 3 October 2011.

How was it possible for Autonomy to leap in value from $6 billion to $7 billion to about $12 billion in a few months in the eyes of HP, even as its CEO was criticized and fired?

To answer the previous question, consider the following questions:

1. What was Autonomy's BATNA? Was it strong or weak?
2. What was HP's BATNA before the press release of 18 August? And after the press release?
3. What was in the press release that informed the world that HP could not reverse course?

Some answers can be found in the HP press releases of 18 August:

- http://h30261.www3.hp.com/phoenix.zhtml?c=71087&p=irol-news Article&ID=1598003

- http://www8.hp.com/emea_africa/en/hp-news/press-release.
  html?id=1051736#.U9UD5PmSzX5

And 3 October:

- http://www8.hp.com/us/en/hp-news/press-release.html?id=1373
  462#.U9b-jvmSw3k

And in these news articles (feel free to search for additional related articles):

- http://www.bloomberg.com/news/2011-08-18/hp-said-to-be-
  near-10-billion-autonomy-takeover-spinoff-of-pc-business.html
- http://fortune.com/2012/11/30/how-hps-meg-whitman-is-passing-
  the-buck

Comments on the H-P Autonomy case

Before the announcement of 18 August, HP had the choice of buying other software companies, though none had seemed so appealing. However, with $13 billion, it could have acquired several smaller companies, looked for other large companies or chosen other ways to make use of the money. Therefore, it had a reasonably strong BATNA.

Autonomy had a weak BATNA – they could continue as an independent company with little organic growth (this was known to HP and other companies that considered acquiring them) or try to make more acquisitions. They were not able to find another company to acquire them. After discussions with various companies in early summer 2011, HP seemed to have the stronger alternatives.

However, after 18 August, Autonomy's weak BATNA was better than HP's. The press release of 18 August showed that HP was betting almost all its money (more than $10 billion of $13 billion total) on one company, at the same time they were starting a major restructuring that would end their PC business and its profits. To Mike Lynch at Autonomy, and most readers of the press release, it seemed that HP had no choice but continue with the acquisition. HP had publicly destroyed their BATNA. Unsurprisingly, Autonomy raised its price.

On top of damaging their own BATNA, HP made it very difficult to stop the transaction because they had too much momentum in the project (full restructuring plus acquisition), as well as ego and credibility at risk among board members. About a year after the acquisition, HP admitted an $8.8 billion loss.

Error: back table out of sync

In the fictitious case that follows, we can see how a manager brought back a result that was unsuitable for and unacceptable to upper management.

Case: Not what the boss really wanted

Alaana informed Jowa of his assignment to complete a deal with Artix, Inc., a customer, for their cooperation in developing an improved version of pallet lifting equipment. She said, "Please negotiate the details with Artix regarding the commitment of hours and staff, as well as the expectations of each side. Above all, we have to keep our costs down and keep ahead of our competitors."

Despite this fairly vague statement of goals, Jowa researched the relationship with Artix, learned about the individuals he would talk with and put together a reasonable agreement committing both sides to exchanges of information, discussions, testing and so on. The agreement put much of the burden for action on Artix and avoided exposing Jowa's company to open commitments of staff and time.

When he brought the draft agreement to Alaana for approval, she looked somewhat annoyed. "You let them take over the project! They will have so much of the inside knowledge that they will not need us." She then negotiated a new agreement without the support of Jowa.

Jowa thought this result was unfair – he had made an agreement that bound Artix to them, not one that would allow the other side to dominate the partnership. However, he realized he had not kept in close enough contact with Alaana. He had let the negotiation get out of contact with the back table.

APPENDIX V

Cultural differences

This appendix contains a few more cultural notes based on the research of Hall, Hofstede, Trompenaars and Hampden-Turner, as well as others. None of these cultural differences can always and reliably be found in any culture; please refer to the discussion in Chapter 4 on culture and stereotyping.

> Review of Chapter 4: culture and behavior expected at a national level does not always apply to individuals, so therefore thinking that all people from one country will behave similarly is false.

Additionally, please consider that experienced negotiators from any country may intentionally neither react nor behave like most people in their home culture.

Showing emotions

Generally, most North Americans, Europeans and people in these language groups show their emotions more obviously than East Asians do; culture researchers call this being affective. Affective means that they are more likely to show that they are frustrated, satisfied, happy, uncomfortable, etc. by speaking or by body language. Although they show emotions easily, they may not be able to read emotions well!

Reading emotions

Generally, the cultures of North America and Northern Europe are low context, which means they may have difficulty reading facial expressions, tone of voice and other body language. They prefer to get information in the form of direct words and phrases.

The result is that affective, low context cultures communicate a lot of information, but cannot read the same information as well from opposite cultures. Therefore, East Asian negotiators may be able to clearly understand the feelings of counterparties from those cultures. But the North American and Northern Europeans may not be able to read the East Asian side.

Advantage for . . .

Unless one side is trying to deceive the other, there is no deep advantage. But there is a strong chance of miscommunication because North Americans and many Europeans could fail to understand the East Asian side. Therefore, the East Asian side should make their feelings about progress, satisfaction, likes and dislikes clearly and explicitly known in words to negotiators from North America and Europe. How? They should try to put their feelings into words, and they should try to use stronger body language with some cultures than they use in their own culture. This process is called accommodating the other side. Do not try to completely accommodate negotiators from other cultures, but do try to be sensitive and a little bit accommodating as you communicate with them. Adjusting in small steps will help the mutual accommodation of all parties.

Too much cultural accommodation

If both sides accommodate too much, no one will be able to correctly understand their words and body language. What to do? Accommodate a little, but not too much. Accommodate more as you become more deeply familiar with local expectations and practices. When you are not sure, ask for information using simple sentences and get advice from individuals with high experience in your culture and the culture you are targeting.

Building trust across cultures in negotiation

Jang and Chua (2011) identify a difficulty that negotiators face when dealing with parties from other cultures. The very behaviors that help you build trust in your culture may cause misunderstanding and mistrust with parties from other cultures. With people from your own cultural background, you know and can use the correct combinations of phrases, the right kind of eye contact, appropriate posture and so on that leads toward trusting relationships. Your idea about this script of actions might, however, lead to the wrong results with people from other backgrounds. In order to manage this process and to learn suitable approaches and scripts of action, Jang and Chua suggest active learning of cultural intelligence (CQ). You can learn more about CQ at http://www.culturalq.com.

Time

People from different cultures may understand time very differently. Most North Americans and many Europeans feel that time must be used "effectively to gain

TABLE A5.1 Misunderstanding perceived value of time

Conversation	Comments
Smith: I can't believe it – we have been talking about this all day with no conclusions!	This negotiator is showing his impatience. Within the US, this would be an easily understood signal that means: "Let's stop wasting time and agree to some concrete details." Outside the US, Smith's words might be misunderstood in many ways.
Tanaka: I see. Can we discuss the part about marketing again?	This negotiator does not recognize the signal from Smith and continues with a slow process.
Smith: Why? We talked about it for 45 minutes! It's clear that you don't care about progress. That's enough. Let's move on to some solid numbers.	Smith gets even more upset.
Tanaka: Ok. Let's move on to the related data. We should analyze this together. It will only take a few hours.	Tanaka seems to understand the need to move on. But he did not communicate his understanding to Smith. Worse, he suggested another long, slow process.
Smith: No. Maybe we should not. I have to visit a company in Taiwan. I hear they like to do business fast.	Smith has given up and ran. Even if we consider Smith too impatient, this is a failure for both Smith and Tanaka.

TABLE A5.2 Improved conversation about time

Conversation	Comments
Smith: I can't believe it – we have been talking about this all day with no conclusions! Tanaka: I see.	This negotiator is showing his impatience.
Smith: OK – I feel that "time is money," but I am willing to discuss . . .	Now Smith knows that Tanaka understands, and the relationship is not in danger of collapse.

progress". In negotiations, they may have limited time available and feel pressure to finish an agreement. Because of this pressure, inexperienced negotiators may give concessions when they get close to their deadline.

In many cases, negotiators with a more flexible idea of time have been able to win significant benefits from negotiators who panicked because of time limits. Experienced negotiators from any culture will not react to time pressure this way – they will manage to avoid time limits. Consider this hypothetical conversation between a US negotiator (Smith) and one from Japan (Tanaka).

Let's improve this conversation so that it becomes a positive event. If Tanaka has enough experience, he will know how to react to Smith. Please write what Tanaka should say and do.

APPENDIX VI

Stakeholder analysis

What is a stakeholder? Stakeholder definitions:

> The Project Management Body of Knowledge (PMBOK) says that a stakeholder is "a person or organization that is actively involved in a project or whose interests are impacted by the execution or completion of a project."
>
> (Project Management Institute, 2013, p. 376)

> A person or organization that has an interest in the project or who could be impacted by it.
>
> (Grisham, 2010, p. 77)

> The people and groups of people who have an interest in the operation and who may be influenced by, or influence, the operation's activities.
>
> (Slack, Brandon-Jones and Johnston, 2013, p. 43)

Central and peripheral stakeholders

It is useful to describe stakeholders based on how active or important they are to a project.

Figure A6.1 shows stakeholders that are central and peripheral to a negotiation course. Please consider who they are and why they are central or peripheral.

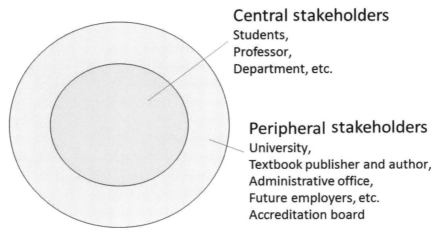

Central stakeholders
Students,
Professor,
Department, etc.

Peripheral stakeholders
University,
Textbook publisher and author,
Administrative office,
Future employers, etc.
Accreditation board

FIGURE A6.1   Central and peripheral stakeholders

Are the lists complete? If not, please identify stakeholders not included previously.

Central	Peripheral
_____	_____
_____	_____
_____	_____

A list of stakeholders should be as broad as possible. Are you a stakeholder in a bridge being built in your town? Probably yes – after all, you and your family pay taxes for that bridge, and you or your visitors and suppliers may use it. With such a broad and open-ended idea about stakeholders, we need to sort the stakeholders in other ways to better understand and react to them.

Power/interest grid

How can we accurately identify some stakeholders as more or less important or powerful, and thereby understand how the project manager should handle them? Figure A6.2 provides a simple tool for assessing and managing stakeholders.

See also page 249 of the PMBOK Guide, Figure 10–4, as well as other comments on analyzing and managing stakeholders, in Chapter 10 of the PMBOK Guide.

Warning – they don't stay in one place!

We have put stakeholders into categories: central, peripheral, high interest, low power, etc. But stakeholders are people, or groups of people, and therefore they can change. A high-interest stakeholder at the start of a project might retain power but lower their interest as the project develops. For example, a bank lending money to

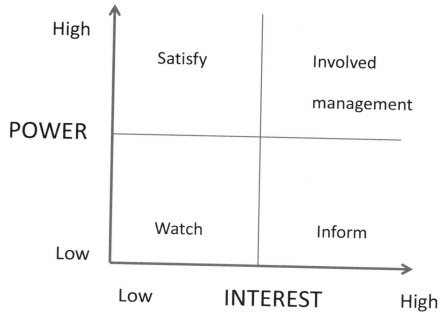

FIGURE A6.2 Power interest grid

TABLE A6.1 Stakeholder analysis, blank

Stakeholder (person, organization, group)	Rights (what they should receive without doubt)	Responsibilities (what they should or must do)	Wants (what they want but do not absolutely need)	Needs (what they must get to be satisfied)	How to handle

a contractor may strongly shape the timing, scale and activities of the contractor, but most of that shaping will happen as the loan is being agreed to. Afterward, the lending bank still retains power, however it is likely to lose interest and unlikely to use that power unless payments are late.

In another example, an environmental activist group may have low power until a project to build a new factory is underway. After the local residents see the earth-moving equipment, they may suddenly join the environmental group, helping to move it from high interest/low power to high interest/high power.

The lesson is this: after you understand the stakeholders on all sides of a negotiation, you must regularly review your information and change your actions toward the stakeholders appropriately.

Use the following case to complete Table A6.1. Answer the "how to handle" column from the point of view of a UK government official. Careful internet searches will provide additional information.

Case: Sensitive foreign investment

In 2014, Huawei, the Chinese electronics maker, made an equity investment in XMOS, a UK technology company. XMOS has several corporate investors including Xilinx (US) and Bosch (Germany). Huawei was blocked from some commercial activities and sales in the United States in 2013 due to the sensitive nature of the top-performing equipment.

XMOS makes semiconductors, especially for the rapidly growing "internet of things". Making a point that Huawei was welcome to participate in this industry in the United Kingdom, the Prime Minister welcomed the company in 2012. The move puts Huawei ahead of competitors in Taiwan and moves them closer to equality with electronics makers from the US and Japan, who already have a strong presence in the UK.

1. Who are the stakeholders in this case?
2. What should be expected from them?
3. What can those stakeholders expect?

Use the stakeholder analysis Table A6.1 to consider the parties and their interests.

REFERENCES

Athabasca University, Faculty of Business. (2013). Table 4.1: Avoiding the weak points of North American negotiators. In Negotiations and Conflict Resolution (LNCR-565) (unpublished course materials). Athabasca University Faculty of Business, St. Albert, Canada.

Bouheraoua, S. and Kulliyyaha, A.I. (2008). Foundation of mediation in Islamic law and its contemporary application. *4th Asia-Pacific Mediation Forum*. Retrieved May 13, 2014 from http://www.asiapacificmediationforum.org/resources/2008/11-_Said.pdf

Bradlow, D. D. and Finkelstein, J. G. (2013). *Negotiating business transactions: An extended simulation course*. Wolters Klouwer: Frederick, MD.

Bressert, S. (2007). What is emotional intelligence (EQ)? *Psych Central*. Retrieved March 8, 2013 from http://psychcentral.com/lib/2007/what-is-emotional-intelligence-eq

Brett, J. (2007). *Negotiating globally* (2nd ed.) [CD included]. John Wiley & Sons: San Francisco, CA.

Brett, J. and Okumura, T. (1998). Inter-and intracultural negotiation: US and Japanese negotiators. *Academy of Management Journal*, 41(5), 495–510.

Browaeys, M. J. and Price, R. (2011). *Understanding Cross-Cultural Management* (2nd ed.). Prentice Hall: Essex, UK.

Burke, C. A. (2010). Mindfulness-based approaches with children and adolescents: A preliminary review of current research in an emergent field. *Journal of Child and Family Studies*, 19(2), 133–144.

Cellich, C. and Jain, S. (2004). *Global business negotiations*. Thomson South-Western: Mason, OH.

Chen, C.-Y. (2008). *How virtual teams use media to manage conflict* (Unpublished doctoral dissertation). University of Manchester, Manchester, UK.

Curhan, J. R., Elfenbein, H. A. and Xu, H. (2006). What do people value when they negotiate? Mapping the domain of subjective value in negotiation. *Journal of Personality and Social Psychology*, 91(3), 493–512.

Davis, I., (n.d.). *Negotiation Techniques in Asian Countries*. USA: Global One. Retrieved January 23, 2015 from http://www.globalonepro.com/go/negotiation-techniques-asian

DeMente, B. L. (2004). *Japan's cultural code words*. Tuttle Publishing: Tokyo.

EDGAR SEC. (2014). Encana Corp: Form 40-F. US Securities and Exchange Commission. Retrieved January 23, 2015 from http://www.sec.gov/Archives/edgar/data/1157806/000110465914011733/a14-4012_240f.htm

Emerson, J. P. (1969). Negotiating the serious import of humor. *Sociometry*, 32(2), 169–181.

Fisher R. and Shapiro, D. (2005). *Beyond reason: Using emotions as you negotiate*. Penguin: New York, NY.

Fisher, R., Ury, W. and Patton, B. (1991). *Getting to yes: Negotiating agreement without giving in*. Houghton Mifflin Harcourt: New York, NY.

Galinsky, A., Maddux, W., Gilin, D. and White, J. (2008). Why it pays to get inside the head of your opponent: The differential effects of perspective taking and empathy in negotiations. *Psychological Science*. 19(4), 378–384.

Global Property Guide. (2014a). Buying costs are very low in Malaysia, August 29. Retrieved January 31, 2015 from http://www.globalpropertyguide.com/Asia/malaysia/Buying-Guide

Global Property Guide. (2014b). Q4 2013: World's Housing Markets in Headlong Boom, Led by U.S. and Asia Pacific, June 5. Retrieved January 31, 2015 from http://www.global propertyguide.com/investment-analysis/Q4-2013-Worlds-housing-markets-in-head long-boom-led-by-US-and-Asia-Pacific

Grisham, T. W. (2010). *International project management: Leadership in complex environments*. Wiley: Hoboken, NJ.

Halpern, J. J. and McLean, J. (1993). Vive la différence: Differences between males and females process and outcomes in a low-conflict negotiation. *International Journal of Conflict Management*, 7(1), 45–70.

Handover, E. (2014). 25 years at the negotiating table. *ACCJ Journal*, 51(8), 23.

Hazeldine, S. (2006). *Bare knuckle negotiating*. Lean Marketing Press: Birmingham, UK.

Hofstede, G. and Hofstede, J. H. (2005). *Cultures and organizations: Software of the mind*. McGraw-Hill: New York, NY.

International Institute for the Unification of Private Law. (2010). *UNIDROIT Principles, 2010*. International Institute for the Unification of Private Law: Rome.

Investopedia. (2015). Royalty Interest. Retrieved January 23, 2015 from http://www.investopedia.com/terms/r/royalty-interest.asp#ixzz1vhIb7jHj

Isaacson, W. (2011). *Steve Jobs*. Little, Brown: London.

Jang, S. and Chua, R. (2011). Building intercultural trust at the negotiating table. In M. Benoliel (Ed.), *Negotiation excellence*. 299–314. World Scientific Publishing: Singapore.

Kahneman, D. (2011). Thinking fast and slow. Farrar, Straus and Giroux: New York, NY.

Kepner, C. H. and Tregoe, B. B. (1997). *The new rational manager*. Princeton Research Press: Skillman, NJ.

Kramarae, C. (2013). *Transform conflict: Mediation resources for Buddhist chaplains* (Unpublished dissertation). Upaya Zen Center/Institute Buddhist Chaplaincy Training Program, NM.

LaFond, C., Vine, S. and Welch, B. (2010). *Negotiation in English*. Oxford University Press: Oxford, UK.

Lavoie, R. (2013). Why-why graphic: Long wait for training. Unpublished document.

Lax, D. and Sebenius, J. (2006). *3D negotiation*. Harvard Business Review Press: Boston, MA.

Lewicki, R. J., Hiam, A. and Olander, K. W. (1996). *Think before you speak: A complete guide to strategic negotiation*. Wiley: Hoboken, NJ.

Li, M. and Sadler, J. (2011). Power and influence in negotiations. In M. Benoliel (Ed.), *Negotiation excellence*. 139–160. World Scientific Publishing: Singapore.

Magill, J. (2012). ConocoPhillips to all but halt new investment in US dry gas plays: CEO. Platts. Retrieved January 20, 2015 from http://www.platts.com/latest-news/natural-gas/washington/conocophillips-to-all-but-halt-new-investment-6279120

Metcalf, H.C. and Bird, A. (2004). Integrating the Hofstede dimensions. In H. Vinken, J. Soeters and P. Ester (Eds.), *Comparing cultures: Dimensions of culture in comparative perspective.* 251–269. Koninklijke Brill BV: Leiden, NL.

Metcalf, H.C., Bird, A., Shankarmahesh, M., Aycan, Z., Larimo, J. and Valdelamar, D. D. (2006). Cultural tendencies in negotiation: A comparison of Finland, India, Mexico, Turkey, and the United States. *Journal of World Business*, 41, 382–394.

Movius, H. and Susskind, L. (2009). *Built to win.* Harvard Business Review Press: Boston.

Hambridge, S. (1995). Netiquette Guidelines. Intel Corp. Retrieved January 19, 2015 from http://www.rfc-editor.org/rfc/rfc1855.txt.

Nisbett, R.E. and Ross, L. (1980). *Human inference: Strategies and shortcomings of social judgment.* Prentice-Hall: Englewood Cliffs, NJ.

Oracle. (2011). Another whopper from Autonomy CEO Mike Lynch. Retrieved July 28, 2014 from http://www.oracle.com/us/corporate/press/503343

Neal, M.A. and Bazerman, M.H. (1985). The effects of framing and negotiator overconfidence on bargaining behaviors and outcomes. *Academy of Management Journal.* 28(1), 34–49.

Nonaka, I. and Takeuchi, H. (1995). *The knowledge-creating company: How Japanese companies create the dynamics of innovation.* Oxford University Press: Oxford, UK.

Ostafin, B. D. and Kassman, K. T. (2012). Stepping out of history: Mindfulness improves insight problem solving. *Consciousness and Cognition*, 21, 1031–1036.

Parker, J. S. and Mosely, J. D. (2008). Kepner-Tregoe decision analysis as a tool to aid route selection, part 1. *Organic Process Research & Development*, 12, 1041–1043.

Pely, D. (2011). Where East not always meet West: Comparing the *sulha* process to Western-style mediation and arbitration. *Conflict Resolution Quarterly*, 28(4), 427–440.

Polanyi, M. (1967). *The tacit dimension.* Routledge and Kegan Paul: London.

Project Management Institute. (2013). A guide to the project management body of knowledge (PMBOK) (5th ed.). PMI: Newtown Square, PA.

Raiffa, H. (2002). *Negotiation analysis: The science and art of collaborative decision making.* Harvard University Press: Cambridge, MA.

Roam, D. (2010). *The back of the napkin.* Penguin: New York, NY.

Salacuse, J.W. (2003). *The global negotiator: Making, managing, and mending deals around the world in the twenty-first century.* Palgrave Macmillan: New York, NY.

Salacuse, J.W. (2004). Negotiating: The top ten ways that culture can affect your negotiation. *Ivey Business Journal.* September/October, 1–6.

Salk, J. and Brannen, M. (2000). National culture, networks, and individual influence in a multinational management team. *Academy of Management Journal*, 43(2), 191–202.

Sato, S. and Urabe, E. (2015, January 8). Lixil weighs takeover for emerging markets push after Grohe. *Bloomberg News.* Retrieved January 20, 2015 from http://www.bloomberg.com/news/2014-01-07/lixil-weighs-deal-for-emerging-markets-push-after-grohe-purchase.html

Sepstrup, S. and Ipsen, L.F. (2013). *Negotiations between Japan & the United States: An analysis of stereotypes and perceptions* (Unpublished bachelor's thesis). Aarhus University, Business and Social Sciences, Denmark.

Sheppard, B. (2003). Negotiating in long-term mutually interdependent relationships among relative equals. In R. Lewicki, D. Saunders, J. Minton and B. Barry (Eds.), *Negotiation: Readings, exercises, and cases.* 264–280. McGraw-Hill: New York, NY.

Slack, N., Brandon-Jones, A. and Johnston, R. (2013). *Operations management* (7th ed.). Pearson Education: Essex, UK.

Subramanian, G. (2010). *Negotiauctions.* W.W. Norton: New York, NY.

Susskind, L. (2013). Can games really change the course of history? *Program on Negotiation.* Retrieved May 4, 2014 from http://www.pon.harvard.edu/research_projects/negotiation-pedagogy-program-on-negotiation/can-games-really-change-the-course-of-history/#!

Swaab, R.I., Postmes, T., Neijens, P., Kiers, M.H. and Dumay, A.C.M. (2002). Multiparty negotiation support: The role of visualization's influence on the development of shared mental models. *Journal of Management Information Systems*, 19(1), 129–150.

Thams, Y., Liu, Y. and von Glinow, M. A. (2013). Asian favors: More than a cookie cutter approach. *Asia Pacific Journal of Management*, 30(2), 461–486.

Thomas, K.W. and Kilmann, R.H. (2007). *Thomas-Kilmann Conflict Mode Instrument*. CPP: Mountain View, CA.

Thompson, L. (2012). *The mind and heart of a negotiator* (5th ed.). Prentice Hall: Upper Saddle River, NJ.

Trompenaars, F. and Hampden-Turner, C. (1998). *Riding the waves of culture*. McGraw-Hill: New York, NY.

US Energy Information Agency (USEIA). (2013). Japan Overview/Data. Retrieved January 2015 from http://www.eia.gov/countries/country-data.cfm?fips=JA

Vuorela, T. (2005). *Approaches to a business negotiation case study: Teamwork, humour, and teaching* (Unpublished dissertation). Helsinki School of Economics, Finland.

Ware, J.P. (1980). *Bargaining strategies: Collaborative versus competitive approaches* (Case Study No. 9–480–055). Harvard Business School Case Services: Boston, MA.

World Intellectual Property Organization (WIPO). (n.d.) http://www.wipo.int/amc/en/mediation. Retrieved January 19, 2015

Additional reading

Moore, C. W. and Woodrow, P. (2010). Handbook of global and multicultural negotiation. Jossey-Bass: San Francisco, CA.

Simons, T. and Tripp, T. (2003). The negotiation checklist. In R. Lewicki, D. Saunders, J. Minton and B. Barry (Eds.), *Negotiation: Sections, exercises, and cases*. pp. 50–63. McGraw-Hill: New York, NY.

INDEX

NOTES

_____
_____
_____
_____
_____
_____
_____
_____
_____
_____
_____
_____
_____
_____
_____
_____
_____
_____
_____
_____

If found, please contact:

Name _____

Tel/email _____